THE

Constitution

— AND THE —

Nation

TEACHING TEXTS IN LAW AND POLITICS

David A. Schultz
General Editor

Vol. 22

PETER LANG
New York • Washington, D.C./Baltimore • Bern
Frankfurt am Main • Berlin • Brussels • Vienna • Oxford

Christopher Waldrep
& Lynne Curry

THE

Constitution

—— AND THE ——

Nation

Establishing the Constitution,
1215–1829

PETER LANG
New York • Washington, D.C./Baltimore • Bern
Frankfurt am Main • Berlin • Brussels • Vienna • Oxford

Library of Congress Cataloging-in-Publication Data

Waldrep, Christopher.
The constitution and the nation. establishing the constitution,
1215–1829 / Christopher Waldrep, Lynne Curry.
p. cm. — (Teaching texts in law and politics; v. 22)
Includes bibliographical references and index.
1. Constitutional history—United States. I. Title: Establishing the
constitution, 1215–1829. II. Curry, Lynne. III. Title. IV. Series.
KF4541.W35   342.73′029—dc21   2002155896
ISBN 0-8204-5730-2
ISSN 1083-3447

Bibliographic information published by **Die Deutsche Bibliothek**.
Die Deutsche Bibliothek lists this publication in the "Deutsche
Nationalbibliografie"; detailed bibliographic data is available
on the Internet at http://dnb.ddb.de/.

Cover design by Lisa Barfield

The paper in this book meets the guidelines for permanence and durability
of the Committee on Production Guidelines for Book Longevity
of the Council of Library Resources.

© 2003 Peter Lang Publishing, Inc., New York
275 Seventh Avenue, 28th Floor, New York, NY 10001
www.peterlangusa.com

Printed in the United States of America

TABLE OF CONTENTS

INTRODUCTION

While few Americans recall details about their Constitution, most have absorbed the great document's basic principles. Some think these principles hopelessly flawed or bigoted, but more treasure the document for its enduring, if perhaps imperfect, values. Together, the four volumes that make up *The Constitution and the Nation* document the changing Constitution, following its intellectual history from a slaveholders' compact to a modern guarantor of individual rights. In other words, we plan to study the Constitution *historically* as the product of change over time. Law is sometimes not studied historically. To anyone at all familiar with the chronologically organized texts that line the walls of any law library, this statement might seem paradoxical. Yet, historians have only studied the law and constitutionalism for three generations. Social and cultural historians even today doubt law really gets at the core of what makes society function. The Constitution often makes only a brief appearance in many U.S. history survey courses.

Law at its most potent presents itself as timeless, immutable, above social change. Law embodies fundamental, unchanging rules. Some lawyers today display the Ten Commandments and evoke Moses in a reflection of such beliefs. History, by contrast, assumes change. History is the study of change over time; other disciplines seek unchanging values, but not history. The political scientist reads Machiavelli to find truths usable in any political situation; the historian reads Machiavelli to learn about the Renaissance. To see law as historical makes powerful assumptions: law does change; law reflects its time; political forces mold law.

A constitution is law, but everyone realizes that constitutional law differs from the sort of law that regulates highway speeds and parking. Constitutional law is fundamental; it is often said to be organic. Constitutional beliefs do not change easily but do change. Americans understand constitution as a construct that restricts power, but constitutions also distribute power, prescribing the extent and manner of the exercise of power. Constitutions also enshrine the society's most basic and cherished beliefs. Without constitutionalism, constitutions are meaningless. Constitutionalism is the belief that the constitution restricts power. For a constitution to effectively limit arbitrary authority, the people must imagine it has force. In the United States, it must be said, constitutionalism is contested. Some Americans genuinely believe their Constitution limits the exercise of power by government and even by the people themselves, but others do not.

The power limited by the Constitution is sovereign, the absolute, unlimited, uncontrollable power by which the state is governed. Federalism is a particular arrangement of power that divides sovereignty between the central authority and regional power centers. The U.S. Constitution divides power between the national government and the states. Readers of this book should remember that it studies the evolution of the distribution of power in the United States.

In editing these documents we have retained original spelling, punctuation, use of italics, and capitalization except when changes proved necessary for sense. For most documents we used original editions, but relied on Avalon for the Magna Carta, which, after all, went through many revisions and iterations.

We must begin also with thanks to all our students who inspired this book with their interest, questions, doubts, and affirmations. We thank the librarians who preserved and located the necessary texts. We must thank also our colleagues who offered suggestions or read portions of the manuscript: Richard B. Bernstein, Newton Key, Sally Hadden, Tim Huebner, and Judy Schafer. Rachel Van helped immeasurably with the preparation of the text for publication.

1.

The Creation of American Constitutionalism

The term *constitutionalism* implies adherence to rules and laws. Within this ideology, a constitution provides a framework of fundamental law upon which governmental structures are built. Another way of viewing a constitution is as a kind of contract, laying out the powers and duties of government on one side and the rights and responsibilities of the governed on the other.

Constitutionalism as an ideology for governing emerged over time. The roots of these ideas extend back several centuries to a system that evolved in England and was already highly developed by the time the first English settlers arrived in the North American colonies. As they established towns and cities in the New World, English men and women brought with them distinct ideas about the ways in which they wanted to govern themselves. Each of the original colonies was founded independently of the others, and over time clear regional, social, economic, and cultural differences among them became apparent. All the colonies, nevertheless, shared two essential founding principles for governance. One was the belief in constitutionalism. The English have a constitution, albeit one that is unwritten, a system of understandings based on certain key documents, including the Magna Carta. The other was the English Common Law, a complex body of laws and punishments that provided the basis for the legal systems that evolved in each of the American colonies.

Each colony operated autonomously, but at the same time each had a contract, or charter, with England that established the rights and responsibilities for each party to the contract. The colonies, therefore, were both independent of each other and tied to a central power, the English Crown and Parliament. A particular model of governance developed in which colonial legislatures shared sovereignty with the central authority. This model is known as *federalism*.

For over one hundred and fifty years, the system worked well for all parties. The colonies grew and prospered, and England benefited from the expansion of its empire into the New World. But this relative calm also had adverse consequences for the authority of England in the colonies. Succeeding generations of Americans grew to regard England as an external government only, necessary for providing defense and regulating intercolonial matters such as trade between the colonies but one that had no authority to interfere in the internal governance of each colony. When Parliament attempted to reassert its powers by enacting new measures taxing and declaring authority in the colonies, many colonists objected. Tensions quickly escalated into violent protests. By the time of the Revolution, Americans argued for a fixed, written constitution that expressly limited the powers of government. The former British colonies, now states, wrote their own constitutions, and the new national legislature produced a separate framework for the central government, the Articles of Convention. The new governing structure preserved the dual-sovereignty model of federalism. In 1787, the states sent representatives to a convention that dramatically revised the structure and functions of the federal government and hammered out a new United States Constitution. For two years Americans debated the merits and flaws of the new framework, contesting the proper balance between state and federal powers. Finally adopted in 1789, this Constitution remains in place today. Like its predecessor the Articles of Confederation, the Constitution reflected Americans' wariness about living under a dominant centralized authority. The 1787 Constitution circumscribed the powers of the federal government, dividing it into three branches and providing a system of checks and balances among the three divisions. Opponents of the Constitution insisted these checks and balances did not go far enough. In 1791, Congress amended the Constitution to provide a separate, enumerated list of protections for the liberties of individual citizens against infringement by the federal government, ten amendments known collectively as the Bill of Rights.

While the powers of the new federal government had been deliberately curbed, the new republic was also established as one unified nation. The central government, therefore, required empowerment to protect, defend, and promote the general welfare of the republic as a whole. States' interests were often at odds with one another, impeding the progress of the nation as a whole. While northern states limited or outlawed the practice of slavery, southern states relied heavily on this labor system, and their laws guarded it carefully. Meanwhile, as Americans continually debated the boundaries between state and federal power, the young nation industrialized, urbanized, took in thousands of immigrants, and pushed its settlers ever westward. New contingencies tested the effectiveness of the Constitution and the continued viability of the federalist model.

Magna Carta (1215)

The Magna Carta, or Great Charter, provides a very early example of the ideology of constitutionalism as it developed in England. Although the monarch's authority to govern came from God, the sovereign's power was circumscribed within a framework of rules and laws. In England, even the king could not rule arbitrarily nor capriciously deny the life, liberty, or property of his subjects. According to English political philosophy, constituted rights also came from God. An examination of the Magna Carta's text reveals its character as a kind of contract between the king and his subjects. Note the level of detail addressed in the agreement. The rights of free Englishmen were carefully guarded.

John, by the grace of God, king of England, lord of Ireland, duke of Normandy and Aquitaine, and count of Anjou, to the archbishop, bishops, abbots, earls, barons, justiciaries, foresters, sheriffs, stewards, servants, and to all his bailiffs and liege subjects, greetings. Know that, having regard to God and for the salvation of our soul, and those of all our ancestors and heirs, and unto the honor of God and the advancement of his holy Church and for the rectifying of our realm, we have granted as underwritten by advice of our venerable fathers, Stephen, archbishop of Canterbury, primate of all England and cardinal of the holy Roman Church, Henry, archbishop of Dublin, William of London, Peter of Winchester, Jocelyn of Bath and Glastonbury, Hugh of Lincoln, Walter of Worcester, William of Coventry, Benedict of Rochester, bishops; of Master Pandulf, subdeacon and member of the household of our lord the Pope, of brother Aymeric (master of the Knights of the Temple in England), and of the illustrious men William Marshal, earl of Pembroke, William, earl of Salisbury, William, earl of Warenne, William, earl of Arundel, Alan of Galloway (constable of Scotland), Waren Fitz Gerold, Peter Fitz Herbert, Hubert De Burgh (seneschal of Poitou), Hugh de Neville, Matthew Fitz Herbert, Thomas Basset, Alan Basset, Philip d'Aubigny, Robert of Roppesley, John Marshal, John Fitz Hugh, and others, our liegemen.

1. In the first place we have granted to God, and by this our present charter confirmed for us and our heirs forever that the English Church shall be free, and shall have her rights entire, and her liberties inviolate; and we will that it be thus observed; which is apparent from this that the freedom of elections, which is reckoned most important and very essential to the English Church, we, of our pure and unconstrained will, did grant, and did by our charter confirm and did obtain the ratification of the same from our lord, Pope Innocent III, before the quarrel arose between us and our barons: and this we will observe, and our will is that it be observed in good faith by our heirs forever. We have also granted to all freemen of our kingdom, for us and our heirs forever, all the underwritten liberties, to be had and held by them and their heirs, of us and our heirs forever....

7. A widow, after the death of her husband, shall forthwith and without difficulty have her marriage portion and inheritance; nor shall she give anything for her dower, or for her marriage portion, or for the inheritance which her husband and she held on the day of the death of that husband; and she may remain in the house of her husband for forty days after his death, within which time her dower shall be assigned to her.

8. No widow shall be compelled to marry, so long as she prefers to live without a husband; provided always that she gives security not to marry without our consent, if she holds of us, or without the consent of the lord of whom she holds, if she holds of another.

9. Neither we nor our bailiffs will seize any land or rent for any debt, as long as the chattels of the debtor are sufficient to repay the debt; nor shall the sureties of the debtor be distrained so long as the principal debtor is able to satisfy the debt; and if the principal debtor shall fail to pay the debt, having nothing wherewith to pay it, then the sureties shall answer for the debt; and let them have the lands and rents of the debtor, if they desire them, until they are indemnified for the debt which they have paid for him, unless the principal debtor can

show proof that he is discharged thereof as against the said sureties....

12. No scutage nor aid shall be imposed on our kingdom, unless by common counsel of our kingdom, except for ransoming our person, for making our eldest son a knight, and for once marrying our eldest daughter; and for these there shall not be levied more than a reasonable aid. In like manner it shall be done concerning aids from the city of London....

14. And for obtaining the common counsel of the kingdom anent the assessing of an aid (except in the three cases aforesaid) or of a scutage, we will cause to be summoned the archbishops, bishops, abbots, earls, and greater barons, severally by our letters; and we will moveover cause to be summoned generally, through our sheriffs and bailiffs, and others who hold of us in chief, for a fixed date, namely, after the expiry of at least forty days, and at a fixed place; and in all letters of such summons we will specify the reason of the summons. And when the summons has thus been made, the business shall proceed on the day appointed, according to the counsel of such as are present, although not all who were summoned have come....

17. Common pleas shall not follow our court, but shall be held in some fixed place....

20. A freeman shall not be amerced for a slight offense, except in accordance with the degree of the offense; and for a grave offense he shall be amerced in accordance with the gravity of the offense, yet saving always his "contentment"; and a merchant in the same way, saving his "merchandise"; and a villein shall be amerced in the same way, saving his "wainage" if they have fallen into our mercy: and none of the aforesaid amercements shall be imposed except by the oath of honest men of the neighborhood.

21. Earls and barons shall not be amerced except through their peers, and only in accordance with the degree of the offense.

22. A clerk shall not be amerced in respect of his lay holding except after the manner of the others aforesaid; further, he shall not be amerced in accordance with the extent of his ecclesiastical benefice....

24. No sheriff, constable, coroners, or others of our bailiffs, shall hold pleas of our Crown....

38. No bailiff for the future shall, upon his own unsupported complaint, put anyone to his "law", without credible witnesses brought for this purposes.

39. No freemen shall be taken or imprisoned or disseised or exiled or in any way destroyed, nor will we go upon him nor send upon him, except by the lawful judgment of his peers or by the law of the land.

40. To no one will we sell, to no one will we refuse or delay, right or justice....

45. We will appoint as justices, constables, sheriffs, or bailiffs only such as know the law of the realm and mean to observe it well....

54. No one shall be arrested or imprisoned upon the appeal of a woman, for the death of any other than her husband.

55. All fines made with us unjustly and against the law of the land, and all amercements, imposed unjustly and against the law of the land, shall be entirely remitted, or else it shall be done concerning them according to the decision of the five and twenty barons whom mention is made below in the clause for securing the pease, or according to the judgment of the majority of the same, along with the aforesaid Stephen, archbishop of Canterbury, if he can be present, and such others as he may wish to bring with him for this purpose, and if he cannot be present the business shall nevertheless proceed without him, provided always that if any one or more of the aforesaid five and twenty barons are in a similar suit, they shall be removed as far as concerns this particular judgment, others being substituted in their places after having been selected by the rest of the same five and twenty for this purpose only, and after having been sworn.

56. If we have disseised or removed Welshmen from lands or liberties, or other things, without the legal judgment of their peers in England or in Wales, they shall be immediately restored to them; and if a dispute arise over this, then let it be decided in the marches by the judgment of their peers; for the

tenements in England according to the law of England, for tenements in Wales according to the law of Wales, and for tenements in the marches according to the law of the marches. Welshmen shall do the same to us and ours....

63. Wherefore we will and firmly order that the English Church be free, and that the men in our kingdom have and hold all the aforesaid liberties, rights, and concessions, well and peaceably, freely and quietly, fully and wholly, for themselves and their heirs, of us and our heirs, in all respects and in all places forever, as is aforesaid. An oath, moreover, has been taken, as well on our part as on the art of the barons, that all these conditions aforesaid shall be kept in good faith and without evil intent. Given under our hand--the above named and many others being witnesses—in the meadow which is called Runnymede, between Windsor and Staines, on the fifteenth day of June, in the seventeenth year of our reign.

Source: http://www.yale.edu/lawweb/avalon/medieval/magframe.htm.

Declaration of Rights (1689)

Massive political struggles in seventeenth-century England resulted in a shift in legal authority from the monarch to the Parliament. English people sought further codification of their individual rights as a means of protection from the kinds of broad and discretionary royal power exercised under the Stuarts, who were overthrown in the "Glorious Revolution." In 1689, a written declaration put forward the rights that the new monarchs, William and Mary, would be bound to respect. A number of the American colonies incorporated the idea of a written list of individual rights into their own charters. The idea of a written list of rights remained powerful one hundred years later when citizens of the new United States of America debated their new Constitution.

Whereas the late King James the Second, by the assistance of divers evil counsellors, judges, and ministers employed by him, did endeavour to subvert and extirpate the Protestant religion and the laws and liberties of this kingdom....

And whereas the said late King James the Second having abdicated the government, and the throne being thereby vacant, his Highness the prince of Orange (whom it hath pleased Almighty God to make the glorious instrument of delivering this kingdom from popery and arbitrary power) did...cause letters to be written to the Lords Spiritual and Temporal being Protestants, and other letters to the several counties, cities, universities, boroughs and cinque ports, for the choosing of such persons to represent them as were of right to be sent to Parliament...in order to such an establishment as that their religion, laws and liberties might not again be in danger of being subverted, upon which letters elections having been accordingly made;

And thereupon the said lords spiritual and temporal and commons...do...(as their ancestors in like case have usually done) for the vindicating and asserting their ancient rights and liberties declare

That the pretended power of suspending the laws or the execution of laws by regal authority without consent of Parliament is illegal.

That the pretended power of dispensing with laws or the execution of laws by regal authority, as it hath been assumed and exercised of late, is illegal.

That the commission for erecting the late Court of Commissioners for Ecclesiastical Causes, and all other commissions and courts of like nature, are illegal and pernicious.

That levying money for or to the use of the Crown by pretence of prerogative, without grant of Parliament, for longer time, or in other manner than the same is or shall be granted, is illegal.

That it is the right of the subjects to petition the king, and all commitments and prosecutions for such petitioning are illegal.

That the raising or keeping a standing army within the kingdom in time of peace, unless it be with consent of Parliament, is against law.

That the subjects which are Protestants may have arms for their defence suitable to their conditions and as allowed by law.

That election of members of Parliament ought to be free.

That the freedom of speech and debates or proceedings in Parliament ought not to be impeached or questioned in any court or place out of Parliament.

That excessive bail ought not to be required, nor excessive fines imposed, nor cruel and unusual punishments inflicted.

That jurors ought to be duly impanelled and returned, and jurors which pass upon men in trials for high treason ought to be freeholders.

That all grants and promises of fines and forfeitures of particular persons before conviction are illegal and void.

And that for redress of all grievances, and for the amending, strengthening and preserving of the laws, Parliaments ought to be held frequently.

And they do claim, demand, and insist upon all and singular the premises, as their undoubted rights and liberties; and that no declarations, judgments, doings or proceedings to the prejudice of the people in any of the said premises ought in any wise to be drawn hereafter into consequence or example....

Source: Danby Pickering, comp., *The Statutes at Large, From the Magna Charta to the end of the 11th Parliament* (London, 1764), 9 :67–69.

Second Treatise of Government (1690)
John Locke

The Enlightenment was a major intellectual movement that swept through elite European circles in the seventeenth and eighteenth centuries. Unwilling to accept that the universe was subject to the mysterious will of God, leaving human beings powerless to change it, Enlightenment thinkers looked for empirical evidence of the workings of nature and sought explanations in terms of rules and laws that could be mastered by the human mind. John Locke was a physician and friend of Sir Isaac Newton who extended Enlightenment ideas about the natural world into the realm of political philosophy. His enormously influential Second Treatise of Government *guided readers through a step-by-step analysis of how men living in a state of absolute freedom in nature voluntarily formed themselves into civil societies ruled by governments and laws. By the mid-eighteenth century, when the American colonists began to question the legitimacy of British authority over their affairs, Locke's assertions about the purpose and respon-*

sibilities of government served as a powerful influence in the shaping of revolutionary ideology.

If Man in the state of Nature be so free as has been said; If he be absolute Lord of his Own Person and Possessions, equal to the greatest, and subject to no Body, why will he part with his Freedom, this Empire, and subject himself to the Dominion and Control of any other Power? To which it is obvious to Answer, that though in the state of Nature he hath such a right, yet the Enjoyment of it is very uncertain, and constantly exposed to the Invasion of others; for all being Kings, as much as he, every Man his Equal, and the greater part no strict Observers of Equity and Justice; the enjoyment of the property he has in this state is very unsafe, very insecure. This makes him willing to quit this Condition, which, however free, is full of fears and continual dangers: and 'tis not without reason, that he seeks out, and is willing to join in Society with others who are already united, or have a mind to unite for the mutual preservation of their Lives, Liberties, and Estates, which I call by the general name, Property.

The great and chief end therefore, of Mens uniting into Commonwealths, and putting themselves under Government, is the preservation of their Property: To which in the state of Nature there are many things wanting.

First, There wants an establish'd, settled, known Law, received and allowed by common consent to be the standard of Right and Wrong, and the common measure to decide all Controversies between them. For though the Law of Nature be plain and intelligible to all rational Creatures, yet Men being biased in their interest, as well as ignorant for want of study of it, are not apt to allow of it as a Law binding to them in the application of it to their particular Cases.

Secondly, In the State of Nature there wants a known and indifferent Judge, with Authority to determine all differences according to the established Law. For every one in that state being both Judge and Executioner of the Law of Nature, Men being partial to themselves, Passion and Revenge is very apt to carry them too far, and with too much heat in their own Cases, as well as negligence and unconcernedness, make them too remiss in other Mens.

Thirdly, In the State of Nature there often wants Power to back and support the Sentence when right, and to give it due Execution. They who by any Injustice offended, will seldom fail, Where they are able, by force to make good their Injustice; such resistance many times makes the punishment dangerous, and frequently destructive to those who attempt it.

Thus Mankind, notwithstanding all the Privileges of the state of Nature, being but in an ill condition while they remain in it are quickly driven into society. Hence it comes to pass, that we seldom find any number of Men live any time together in this State. The inconveniences that they are therein exposed to, by the irregular and uncertain exercise of the Power every Man has of punishing the transgressions of others, make them take Sanctuary under the establish'd laws of Government, and therein seek the preservation of their Property. 'Tis this makes them so willingly give up every one his single power of punishing to be exercised by such alone as shall be appointed to it amongst them; and by such Rules as the Community, or those authorised by them, to that purpose shall agree on. And in this we have the original right and rise of both the Legislative and Executive Power, as well as of the Governments and Societies themselves.

For in the state of Nature, to omit the liberty he has of innocent delights, a Man has two Powers. The first is to do whatsoever he thinks fit for the preservation of himself and others within the permission of the Law of Nature; by which Law, common to them all, he and all the rest of Mankind, are one Community, make up one Society distinct from all other Creatures, and were it not for the corruption and viciousness of degenerate Men, there would be no need of any other, no necessity that men should separate from this great and natural Community, and associate into lesser Combinations. The other power a man has in the state of Nature is the power to punish the Crimes committed against that Law. Both these he gives up when he joins in a private, if I may so call it, or particular Political Society, and incorporates into any Commonwealth, separate from the rest of Mankind.

The first power, *viz.* of doing whatsoever he thought fit for the preservation of himself, and the rest of Mankind, he gives up to be regulated by Laws made by the Society, so far forth as the preservation of himself and the rest of that Society shall require; which Laws of the Society in many things confine the liberty he had by the Law of Nature.

Secondly, the power of punishing he wholly gives up, and engages his natural force, which he might before employ in the Execution of the Law of Nature, by his own single Authority, as he thought fit, to assist the Executive Power of the Society, as the Law thereof shall require. For being now in a new State, wherein he is to enjoy many Conveniences from the labour, assistance, and society of others in the same Community, as well as the protection from its whole strength, he is to part also with as much of his natural liberty, in providing for himself, as the good, prosperity and safety of the Society shall require; which is not only necessary but just, since the other Members of Society do the like.

But though Men when they enter into Society give up the Equality, Liberty, and Executive Power they had in the state of Nature, into the hands of the society, to be so far disposed of the Legislative, as the good of Society shall require; yet it being only with an intention in every one, the better to preserve himself, his Liberty and Property (For no rational Creature can be supposed to change his condition with the intention to be worse) the power of the Society or Legislative, constituted by them, can never be supposed to extend farther than the common good; but is obliged to secure every ones property by providing against those three defects above mentioned, that made the state of Nature so unsafe and uneasy. And so whoever has the Legislative or Supreme Power of any Commonwealth, is bound to govern by established standing Laws, promulgated and known to the People, and not by Extemporary Decrees; By indifferent and upright Judges, who are to decide Controversies by those Laws. And to employ the force of the Community at home, only in the Execution of such Laws, or abroad to prevent or redress foreign Injuries and secure the Community from Inroads and Invasion. And all this to be directed to no other end, but the Peace, Safety, and public good of the People.

Source: John Locke, *Two Treatises of Government* (London, 1690), 345–350.

Cato's Letters (1720–1723)

John Trenchard and Thomas Gordon, writing as "Cato," published a series of letters in the London Journal *that reflected contemporary political debates among English people. Trenchard and Gordon represented the opposition in England: they favored replacing the monarchy with a republican form of government. Trenchard was a member of the Whig Party and briefly served as a member of Parliament. Few in England took them seriously; most thought the Glorious Revolution had resolved the problems Trenchard and Gordon made the subject of their newspaper columns. But while the citizens of England largely ignored Trenchard and Gordon, their writings would later have great influence in the colonies. In the following selections, "Cato" asserts the crucial importance of preserving individual liberties in order to prevent government from becoming tyrannical. The letters were widely available in the North American colonies and were published in a single volume in 1724. The essays of Trenchard and Gordon helped to provide the colonists with a conceptual framework and a political vocabulary as they debated issues of liberty and power on the eve of the Revolution.*

Letter No. 15.

SATURDAY, *February* 4, 1720

*Of Freedom of Speech: That the same is inseparable
from publick Liberty.*

SIR,

WITHOUT Freedom of Thought, there can be no such thing as wisdom; and no such Thing as Wisdom; and no such Thing as publick Liberty, without freedom of speech; which is the Right of every Man, as far as by it he does not hurt or controul the Right of another; and this is the only Check which it ought to suffer, the only Bounds which it ought to know.

This sacred privilege is so essential to free Governments, that the Security of Property, and the Freedom of Speech, always go together; and in those wretched Countries where a Man cannot call his Tongue his own, he can scarce call any Thing else his own. Whoever would overthrow the Liberty of a Nation, must begin by subduing the Freedom of Speech; a Thing terrible to publick Traitors.

This Secret was so well known to the Court of King *Charles* the First, that his wicked Ministry procured a Proclamation, to forbid the People to talk of Parliaments, which those Traitors had laid aside. To assert the undoubted Right of the Subject, and defend his Majesty's legal Prerogative, was called Disaffection, and punished as sedition. Nay, people were forbid to talk of Religion in their families....

The Administration of Government, is nothing else but the Attendance of the Trustees the People upon the Interest and Affairs of the People; And as it is the Part and Business of the People, for whose Sake alone all publick Matters are or ought to be transacted, to see whether they be well or ill transacted; so it is the Interest, and ought to be the Ambition, of honest Magistrates, to have their Deeds openly examined, and publickly scanned: Only wicked Governors of Men dread what is said of them....

Freedom of Speech is ever the Symptom, as well as the Effect, of good Government....

Letter No. 17

SATURDAY, *February* 18, 1720

What Measures are actually taken by wicked and desperate Ministers to ruin and enslave their Country.

SIR,

As under the best Princes, and the best Servants to Princes alone, it is safe to speak what is true of the worst; so, according to my former Promise to the Publick, I shall take the Advantage of our excellent King's most gentle Government, and the virtuous Administration of an uncorrupt Ministry, to warn Mankind against the Mischiefs which may hereafter be dreaded from corrupt ones. It is too true, that every Country in the World has sometimes groaned under that heavy Misfortune, and our own as much as any; though I cannot allow it to be true, what Monsieur *de Witt* has long since observed, that the *English* court has always been the most thievish court in *Europe*.

Few Men have been desperate enough to attack openly, and barefaced, the Liberties of a free People. Such avowed Conspirators can rarely succeed: The Attempt would destroy itself. Even when the Enterprize is begun and visible, the End must be hid, or denied. It is the Business and Policy of Traitors, so to disguise their Treason with plausible Names, and so to recommend it with popular and bewitching Colours, that they themselves shall be adored, while their Work is detested, and yet carried on by those that detest it.

Thus one Nation has been surrendered to another under the fair Name of mutual Alliance: The Fortresses of a Nation have been given up, or attempted to be given up, under the frugal Notion of saving Charges to a Nation; and Commonwealths have been trepanned into Slavery, by Troops raised or increased to defend them from slavery.

It may therefore be of Service to the World, to shew what Measures have been taken by corrupt Ministers, in some of our neighbouring Countries, to ruin and enslave the People over whom they presided; to shew by what Steps and Gradations of Mischief Nations have been undone, and consequently what Methods may be hereafter taken to undo others: and this Subject I rather choose, because my Countrymen may be the more sensible of, and know how to value, the inestimable Blessing of living under the best Prince, and the best established Government in the Universe, where we have none of these Things to fear.

Such Traitors will probably endeavour first to get their Prince into their Possession, and, like *Sejanus*, shut him up in a little Island, or perhaps make him a Prisoner in his Court; whilst, with full Range, they devour his Dominions, and plunder his Subjects. When he is thus secluded from the Access of his Friends, and the Knowledge of his Affairs, he must be content with such Misrepresentations as they shall find expedient to give him. False Cases will be stated, to justify wicked Counsel; wicked Counsel will be given, to procure unjust Orders. He will be made to mistake his Foes for his Friends, his Friends for his Foes; and to believe that his Affairs are in the highest Prosperity, when they are in the greatest Distress, and that publick Matters go on in the greatest Harmony, when they are in the utmost Confusion.

They will be ever contriving and forming wicked and dangerous Projects, to make the People poor, and themselves rich; well knowing that Dominion follows Property; that where there are Wealth and Power, there will be always Crowds of servile Dependents; and that, on the contrary, Poverty dejects the Mind, fashions it for Slavery, and renders it unequal to any generous Undertaking, and incapable of opposing any bold Usurpation. They will squander away the publick Money in wanton Presents to Minions, and their Creatures of Pleasure, or of Burden, or in Pensions to mercenary and worthless Men and Women, for vile Ends, and traitorous Purposes.

They will engage their Country in ridiculous, expensive, fantastical Wars, to keep the Minds of Men in continual Hurry and Agitation, and under constant Fears and Alarms; and by such Means deprive them both of Leisure and Inclination to look into publick Miscarriages. Men, on the contrary, will, instead of such Inspection, be disposed to fall into all Measures offered, seemingly, for their defence, and will agree to every wild Demand made by those who are betraying them.

When they have served their Ends by such Wars, or have other Motives to make Peace, they will have no View to the publick Interest; but will often, to procure such Peace, deliver up the Strong Holds of their Country, or its Colonies for Trade, suspected

Friends, or dangerous Neighbours, that they may not be interrupted in their Domestick Designs.

They will create Parties in the Commonwealth, or keep them
up where they already are; and by playing them by Turns upon
each other, will rule both. By making the *Guelfs* afraid of the
Ghibelines, and these afraid of the *Guelfs*, they will make them
selves the Mediums and Balance between the two Factions; and
both Factions, in their Turns, the props of their Authority, and the
Instruments of their Designs.

They will not suffer any Men, who have once tasted of Authority, though personally their Enemies, and whose Posts they
enjoy, to be called to an Account for past Crimes, though ever so
enormous. They will make no such Precedents for their own Punishment, nor censure Treason, which they intend to commit. On
the contrary, they will form new Conspiracies, and invent new
Fences for their own Impunity and Protection; and endeavour to
engage such Numbers in their Guilt, as to set themselves above all
Fear of Punishment.

They will prefer worthless and wicked Men, and not suffer a
Man of Knowledge or Honesty to come near them, or enjoy a Post
under them. They will disgrace Men of Virtue, and ridicule Virtue
itself, and laugh at publick Spirit. They will put Men into Employments, without any Regard to the Qualifications for these
Employments, or indeed to any Qualification at all, but as they
contribute to their Designs, and shew a stupid Alacrity to do what
they are bid. They must be either Fools or Beggars; either void of
Capacity to discover their Intrigues, or of Credit and Inclination to
disappoint them.

They will promote Luxury, Idleness, and Expence, and a gen-
eral Depravation of Manners, by their own Example, as well as by
Connivance and publick Encouragement. This will not only divert
Men's Thoughts from examining their Behaviour and Politicks,
but likewise let them loose from all the Restraints of private and
publick Virtue. From Immorality and Excesses, they will fall into
Necessity; and from thence into a servile Dependence upon
Power.

In order to this, they will bring into Fashion Gaming, Drunkenness, Gluttony, and profuse and costly Dress. They will debauch their Country with foreign Vices, and foreign Instruments of vicious Pleasures; and will contrive and encourage publick Revels, nightly Disguises, and debauched Mummeries.

They will, by all practicable Means of Oppression, provoke the People to Disaffection; and then make that Disaffection an Argument for new Oppression, for not trusting them any further, and for keeping up Troops; and, in fine, for depriving them of Liberties and Privileges, to which they are entitled by their Birth, and the Laws of their Country.

If such Measures should ever be taken in any free Country, where the People choose Deputies to represent them, then they will endeavour to bribe the Electors in the Choice of their Representatives, and so to get a Council of their own Creatures; and where they cannot succeed with the Electors, they will endeavour to corrupt the Deputies after they are chosen, with the Money given for the publick Defence; and to draw into the Perpetration of their Crimes those very Men, from whom the betrayed People expect the Redress of their Grievances, and the Punishment of those Crimes. And when they have thus made the Representatives of the People afraid of the People, and the People afraid of their Representatives; then they will endeavour to persuade those Deputies to seize the Government to themselves, and not to trust their Principals any longer with the Power of resenting their Treachery and ill Usage, and of sending honester and wiser Men in their Room.

But if the Constitution should be so stubbornly framed, that it will still preserve itself and the People's Liberties, in spite of all villainous Contrivances to destroy both; then must the Constitution itself be attacked and broken, because it will not bend. There must be an Endeavour, under some Pretence of publick Good, to alter a Balance of the Government, and to get it into the sole power of their Creatures, and of such who will have constantly an Interest distinct from that of the Body of the People.

But if all these Schemes for the Ruin of the Publick, and their own Impunity, should fail them; and the worthy Patriots of a free

Country should prove obstinate in Defence of their Country, and resolve to call its Betrayers to a strict Account; there is then but one Thing left for such Traitors to do; namely, to veer about, and by joining with the Enemy of their Prince and Country, complete their Treason.

I have somewhere read of a Favourite and first Minister to a neighbouring Prince, long since dead, who played his Part so well, that, though he had, by his evil Counsels, raised a Rebellion, and a Contest for the Crown; yet he preserved himself a Resource, whoever got the better: If his old Master succeeded, then this *Achitophel*, by the Help of a baffled Rebellion, ever favourable to Princes, had the glory of fixing his Master in absolute Power: But, as his brave Rival got the Day, *Achitophel* had the merit of betraying his old Master to plead; and was accordingly taken into Favour....

Letter No. 31

SATURDAY, *May* 27, 1721

Considerations on the Weakness and Inconsistencies
of human Nature.

SIR,

THE Study of human Nature has, ever since I could study any Thing, been a principal Pleasure and Employment of mine; a Study as useful, as the Discoveries made by it are for the most part melancholy. It cannot but be irksome to a good-natured Man, to find that there is nothing so terrible or mischievous, but human Nature is capable of it; and yet he who knows little of human Nature, will never know much of the Affairs of the World, which every where derive their Motion and Situation from the Humours and Passions of Men.

It shews the violent Bent of human Nature to Evil, that even the Christian Religion has not been able to tame the restless Appetites of Men, always pushing them into Enormities and Violences, in direct Opposition to the Spirit and Declarations of the Gospel, which commands us to *do unto all Men what we would have all Men do unto us.* The general Practice of the World is an open Contradiction and Contempt of this excellent, this divine Rule; which alone, were it observed, would restore Honesty and Happiness to Mankind, who, in their present State of Corruption, are for ever dealing treacherously or outrageously with one another, out of an ill-judging Fondness for themselves.

Nay, the peaceable, the beneficent, the forgiving Christian Religion, is made the cause of perpetual Hatred, Animosity, Quarrels, Violence, Devastation, and Oppression; and the Apostles, in spite of all their Poverty, Disinterestedness, and Love of Mankind, are made to justify their pretended Successors of the Church of *Rome*, in engrossing to themselves the Wealth and Power of the Earth; and in bringing Mankind under a Yoke of Servitude, more terrible, more expensive, and more severe, than all the Arts and Delusions of Paganism could ever bring them under: Of so much more Force with the corrupt World, are the destructive Villainies and Falsifications of Men, than the benevolent and heavenly Precepts of Jesus Christ.

The Truth is, and it is a melancholy Truth, that where human Laws do not tie Men's Hands from Wickedness, Religion too seldom does; and the most certain Security which we have against Violence, is the Security of the Laws. Hence it is, that the making of Laws supposes all Men naturally wicked; and the surest Mark of Virtue is, the Observation of Laws that are virtuous: If therefore we would look for Virtue in a Nation, we must look for it in the Nature of Government; the Name and Model of their Religion being no certain Symptom nor Cause of their Virtue. The *Italians* profess the Christian Religion, and the *Turks* are all Infidels; are the *Italians* therefore more virtuous than the *Turks*? I believe no body will say that they are; at least those of them that live under Absolute Princes: On the contrary, it is certain, that as the Subjects of the Great *Turk* are not more miserable than those of the Pope, so neither are they more wicked.

Of all the Passions which belong to human Nature, *Self-love* is the strongest, and the Root of all the rest; or, rather, all the different Passions are only several Names for the several Operations of Self-love; *Self-love*, says the Duke of *Rochefoucault, is the Love of one's self, and of every Thing else for one's own Sake: It makes a Man the Idolater of himself, and the Tyrant of others.* He observes, that Man is a Mixture of Contrarieties, imperious and supple, sincere and false, fearful and bold, merciful and cruel: He can sacrifice every Pleasure to the getting of Riches, and all his Riches to a Pleasure: He is fond of his Preservation, and yet sometimes eager after his own Destruction: He can flatter those whom he hates, destroy those whom he loves.

This is a Picture of Mankind; and they who say it is a false one, ought to shew that they deserve a better. I have sometimes thought, that it was scarce possible to assert any thing concerning Mankind, be it ever so good, or ever so evil, but it will prove true. They are naturally Innocent, yet fall naturally into the Practice of Vice; the greatest Instances of Virtue and Villainy are to be found in one and the same Person; and perhaps one and the same Motive produces both. The Observance or Non-observance of a few frivolous Customs, shall unite them in strict Friendship and Confederacy, or set them a cutting one another's throats....

Letter No. 33

SATURDAY *June* 17, 1721.

Cautions against the natural Encroachments of Power.

SIR,

...Political Jealousy...in the People, is a necessary and laudable Passion. But in a chief Magistrate, a Jealousy of his People is not so justifiable, their Ambition being only to preserve themselves; whereas it is natural for Power to be striving to enlarge itself, and to be encroaching upon those that have none. The most laudable Jealousy of a Magistrate is to be jealous *for* his People; which will shew that he loves them, and has used them well: But to be jealous *of* them, would denote that he has evil Designs against them, and has used them ill. The People's Jealousy tends to preserve Liberty; and the Prince's to destroy it. *Venice* is a glorious Instance of the former, and so is *England*; and all Nations who have lost their Liberty, are melancholy Proofs of the latter.

Power is naturally active, vigilant and distrustful; which Qualities in it push it upon all Means and Expedients to fortify itself, and upon destroying all Opposition, and even all Seeds of Opposition, and make it restless as long as any thing stands in its Way. It would do what it pleases, and have no Check. Now, because Liberty chastises and shortens Power, therefore Power would extinguish Liberty; and consequently Liberty has too much Cause to be exceeding jealous, and always upon her Defence. Power has many Advantages over her; it has generally numerous Guards, many Creatures, and much Treasure; besides, it has more Craft and Experience, less Honesty and Innocence: And whereas Power can, and for the most part does subsist where Liberty is not, Liberty cannot subsist without Power; so that she has, as it were, the Enemy always at her Gates.

Some have said, that Magistrates being accountable to none but God, ought to know no other Restraint. But this Reasoning is as frivolous as it is wicked; for no good Man cares how many Punishments and Penalties lie in his Way to an Offence which he does not intend to commit: A Man who does not mean to commit Murder, is not sorry that Murder is punished with Death. And as to wicked Men, their being accountable to God, whom they do not fear, is no Security to use against their Folly and Malice; and to say that we ought to have no Security against them, is to insult common Sense, and give the Lie to the first Law of Nature, that of Self-Preservation. Human Reason says, that there is no Obedience, no Regard due to those Rulers, who govern by no Rule but their Lust: Such Men are no Rulers; they are Outlaws; who, being at Defiance with God and Man, are protected by no Law of God, or of Reason. By what Precept, moral or divine, are we forbid to kill a Wolf, or burn an infected Ship? Is it unlawful to prevent Wickedness and Misery, and to resist the Authors of them? Are Crimes sanctified by their Greatness? And is he who robs a Country, and murders Ten Thousand, less a Criminal than he who steals single

Guineas, and takes away single Lives? Is there any Sin in preventing, and restraining, or resisting the greatest Sin that can be committed, that of oppressing and destroying Mankind by wholesale? Sure there never were such open, such shameless, such selfish Impostors, as the Advocates for lawless Power! It is a damnable Sin to oppress Them; yet it is a damnable Sin to oppose them when They Oppress, or gain by Oppression of others. When they are hurt themselves ever so little, or but think themselves hurt, they are the loudest of all Men in their Complaints, and the most outrageous in their Behaviour: But when others are plundered, oppressed and butchered, Complaints are Sedition; and to seek Redress, is Damnation. Is not this to be the Authors of all Wickedness and Falsehood?

To conclude: Power, without Control, appertains to God alone; and no Man ought to be trusted with what no Man is equal to. In Truth there are so many Passions, and Inconsistencies, and so much Selfishness, belonging to human Nature, that we can scarce be too much upon our Guard against each other. The only Security which we can have that Men will be honest, is to make it their Interest to be honest; and the best Defence which we can have against their being Knaves, is to make it terrible to them to be Knaves. As there are many Men wicked in some Stations, who would be innocent in others; the best Way is to make Wickedness unsafe in any Station....

Source: Cato's Letters of Essays on Liberty, Civil and Religious, 4 vols. (London: 1733), 1:96-97, 111–117, 237–239, 260–263.

Commentaries on the Laws of England (1765)
William Blackstone

Along with the ideology of constitutionalism, Americans brought the traditions of the English Common Law to their New World settlements. William Blackstone's masterwork, Commentaries on the Laws of England, *delineates and explains this complex body of laws. Although Blackstone wrote in the eighteenth century, his Commentaries remained the authoritative source on Common Law in the United States well into the nineteenth century. In the following selection, Blackstone describes the theoretical underpinnings of British constitutionalism, which for Blackstone represents the best of the three principal archetypes of governance as described by "the ancients." Blackstone's weighing of the strengths and weaknesses of democracy, aristocracy, and monarchy resonated with American colonists in the Revolutionary era as they considered their own problems with the British government in addition to the possibility of replacing British rule with a completely different form of government.*

...But happily for us of this island,...the executive power of the laws is lodged in a single person, they have all the advantages of strength and dispatch, that are to be found in the most absolute monarchy; and, as the legislature of the kingdom is entrusted to three distinct powers, entirely independent of each other, first, the king, secondly, the lords spiritual and temporal, which is an aristocratical assembly of persons selected for their piety, their birth, their wisdom, their valour, or their property; and, thirdly, the house of commons, freely chosen by the people from among themselves, which makes it a kind of democracy; as this aggregate body, actuated by different sprints, and attentive to different interests composes, the British parliament, and has the supreme disposal of every thing; there can no inconvenience be attempted by either of the three branches, but will be withstood by one of the other two; each branch being armed with a negative power, sufficient to repel any innovation which it shall think inexpedient or dangerous.

Here then is lodged the sovereignty of the British constitution; and lodged as beneficially as is possible for society. For in no other shape could we be for certain of finding the three great qualities of governments so well and so happily united. If the supreme power were lodged in any one of the three branches separately, we must be exposed to the inconveniences of either absolute monarchy, aristocracy, or democracy; and so want two of the three principal ingredients of good polity, either virtue, wisdom, or power....the constitutional government of this island is so admirably tempered and compounded, that nothing can endanger or hurt it, but destroying the equilibrium of power between one branch of the legislature and the rest....

Source: William Blackstone, *Commentaries on the Laws of England* (Oxford, 1765), 1:50.

The Wealth of Nations (1776)
Adam Smith

The American colonists also read and were enormously influenced by Adam Smith's economic treatise on the capitalist system, The Wealth of Nations. *Like his contemporaries who wrote about political theory, Smith thought about the problem of liberating the individual and keeping government power in check. For Smith, capitalism provided the foundation for liberty because, unlike the entrenched landed aristocracies of Europe, the rational market system rewarded individuals for their initiative and effort, thus creating the greatest good for the greatest number. The best government, therefore, was the government that interfered least with the workings of the private economy. After the Revolution, the American republican experiment would be inextricably linked with the development of free market capitalism.*

Inequalities Occasioned by the Policy of Europe

...the policy of Europe, by not leaving things at perfect liberty, occasions other inequalities....

It does this chiefly in the three following ways. First, by restraining the competition in some employments to a smaller number than would otherwise be disposed to enter into them; secondly, by increasing it in others beyond what it naturally would be; and, thirdly, by obstructing the free circulation of labour and stock, both from employment to employment and from place to place.

First, the policy of Europe occasions a very important inequality in the whole of the advantages and disadvantages of the different employments of labour and stock, by restraining the competition in some employments to a smaller number than might otherwise be disposed to enter into them....

The property which every man has in his own labour, as it is the original foundation of all other property, so it is the most sacred and inviolable. The patrimony of a poor man lies in the strength and dexterity of his hands; and to hinder him from employing the strength and dexterity in what manner he thinks proper without injury to his neighbour, is a plain violation of this most sacred property. It is a plain violation of this most sacred property. It is a manifest encroachment upon the just liberty both of the workman, and of those who might be disposed to employ him. As it hinders the one from working at what he thinks proper, so it hinders the others from employing whom they think proper. To judge whether he is fit to be employed, may surely be trusted to the discretion of employers whose interest it so much concerns. The affected anxiety of the lawgiver lest they should employ an improper person, is evidently as impertinent as it is oppressive....

Source: Adam Smith, *An Inquiry into the Nature and Causes of the Wealth of Nations,* 3 vols. (Philadelphia, 1789), 1:156–161.

A Vindication of the Rights of Woman (1792)
Mary Wollstonecraft

In the revolutionary atmosphere of the late eighteenth and early nineteenth centuries, many intellectuals probed the question of whether human beings were innately capable of governing themselves. Thus the "true nature of man" became a topic of utmost concern. The British writer Mary Wollstonecraft asserted that a successful republic required the contributions of both men and women to the public arena. But women's legal, economic, and social dependence on men kept them from taking their place alongside men. Wollstonecraft blasted the European conventions that restricted women's world to the minutiae of everyday life, rendering them perpetually petty, selfish, and child-like. While not an overt call to a feminist revolution, Wollstonecraft's essay insisting that women be allowed to develop fully as individuals independent of men was quite radical in its implications and would serve as a crucial touchstone for later generations of European and American feminists.

From the tyranny of man, I firmly believe, the greater number of female follies proceed; and the cunning, which I allow makes at present a part of their character, I likewise have repeatedly endeavoured to prove, is produced by oppression....

Asserting the rights which women in common with men ought to contend for, I have not attempted to extenuate their faults; but to prove them to be the natural consequence of their education and station in society. If so, it is reasonable to suppose that they will change their character, and correct their vices and follies, when they are allowed to be free in a physical, moral, and civil sense.

Let woman share the rights and she will emulate the virtues of man; for she must grow more perfect when emancipated, or justify the authority that chains such a weak being to her duty. If the latter, it will be expedient to open a fresh trade with Russia for whips; a present which a father should always make to his son-in-law on his wedding day, that a husband may keep his whole family in order by the same means; and without any violation of justice reign, wielding this sceptre, sole master of his house, because he is the only being in it who has reason;--the divine, indefeasible earthly sovereignty breathed into man by the Master of the universe. Allowing this position, women have not any inherent rights to claim; and, by the same rule, their duties vanish, for rights and duties are inseparable.

Be just then, O ye men of understanding, and mark not more severely what women do amiss, than the vicious tricks of the horse or ass for whom ye provide provender--and allow her the privileges of ignorance, to whom ye deny the rights of reason, or ye will be worse than Egyptian taskmasters, expecting virtue where nature has not given understanding!

Source: Mary Wollstonecraft, *A Vindication of the Rights of Woman with Strictures on Political and Moral Subjects* (London, 1891), 285–287.

2.

The North American Colonies

English settlers brought to the North American Colonies their own distinct ideas about the nature and purpose of government, drawn from long-standing traditions of constitutionalism and the English Common Law. But North America was not England, and the settlers inevitably found themselves facing new contingencies that required modifications in their Old World legal traditions. While each step away from England may have seemed of little significance at the time, the sum total of these changes ultimately led to revolution. The documents in this chapter represent the evolution of constitutionalism in America, shaped over several generations by the particular social, economic, geographic, and political context of life in the colonies.

Lawes, Divine, Morall, and Martiall for the Colony of Virginia (1612)

From its founding in 1607, the English settlement at Jamestown proved to be an extremely difficult and unprofitable enterprise for the merchants of the Virginia Company. In 1612, the Virginia Colony's governor, Thomas Dale, faced considerable pressure from investors to whip the colony into shape. The Lawes, Divine, Morall, and Martiall represented an attempt to bring law and order to the settlement by regulating myriad aspects of individuals' daily lives. As this excerpt shows, the proscriptions for behavior and the proposed punishments for violators were intended to demonstrate that very little disorder would be tolerated.

2. ....That no man speake impiously or maliciously, against the holy and blessed Trinitie, or any of the three persons, that is to say, against God the Father, God the Son, and God the holy Ghost, or against the knowne Articles of the Christian faith, upon paine of death.

3. That no man blaspheme Gods holy name upon paine of death, or use unlawful oathes, taking the name of God in vaine, curse, or banne, upon paine of severe punishment for the first offence so committed, and for the second, have a bodkin thrust through his tongue, and if he continue the blaspheming of Gods holy name, for the third time so offending, he shall be brought to a martiall court, and there receive censure of death for his offence.

4. No man shall use any traiterous words against his Majesties Person, or royall authority upon paine of death....

6. Everie man and woman duly twice a day upon the first towling of the Bell shall upon the working daies repaire unto the Church, to hear divine Service upon pain of losing his or her dayes allowance for the first omission, for the second to be whipt, and for the third to be condemned to the Gallies for the six Moneths. Likewise no man or woman shall dare to violate or breake the Sabboth by any gaming, publique, or private abroade, or at home, but duly sanctifie and observe the same, both himselfe and his famlie, by preparing themselves at home with private prayer, that they may be the better fitted for the

publique, according to the commandements of God, and the orders of our Church, as also every man and woman shall repaire in the morning to the divine service, and Sermons preached upon the Sabboth day, and in the afternoon to divine service, and Catechising....

13. No manner of Person whatsoever, contrarie to the word of God (which tyes every particular and private man, for conscience sake to obedience, and duty of the Magistrate, and such as shall be placed in authoritie over them, shall detract, slaunder, calumniate, murmur, mutenie, resist, disobey, or neglect the commaundments, either of the Lord Governour, and Captaine Generall, the Lieutenant Generall, the Martiall, the Councell, or any authorised Captaine, Commaunder or publike Officer, upon pain for the first time so offending to be whipt three severall times, and upon his knees to acknowledge his offence, with asking forgiveness upon the Sabboth day in the assembly of the congregation, and for the second time so offending to be condemned to the Gally for three years: and for the third time so offending to be punished with death.

14. No man shall give any disgraceful words, or commit any act to the disgrace of any person in this Colonie, or any part thereof, upon paine of being tied head and feete together, upon the guard everie night for the space of one moneth, besides to bee publikely disgraced himselfe, and be made uncapable ever after to possesse any place, or execute any office in this imployment.

15. No man of what condition soever shall barter, trucke, or trade with the Indians, except he be thereunto appointed by lawful authority, upon paine of death....

22. There shall be no man or woman, Launderer or Launderesse, dare to wash any uncleane Linnen, drive bucks, or throw out the water or suds of fowle cloathes, in the open streete, within the Pallizadoes, or within forty foote of the same, nor rench, and make cleane, kettle, pot, pan, or such like vessell within twenty foote of the olde well, or new Pumpe: nor shall any one aforesaid, within less then a quarter of one mile from the Pallizadoes, doare to doe the necessites of nature, since by these

unmanly, slothfull, and loathsome immodesties, the whole Fort may bee choaked, and poisoned with ill aires, and so corrupt (as in all reason cannot but much infect the same) and this shall they take notice of, and avoide, upon paine of whipping and further punishment, as shall be thought meete, by the censure of a martiall Court....

31. What man or woman soever, shall rob any garden, publike or private, being set to weed the same, or wilfully pluck up therein any roote, herbe, or flower, to spoile and wast or steale the same, or robbe any vineyard, or gather up the grapes, or steale any eares of the corne growing, whether in the ground belongings to the same fort or towne where he dwelleth, or in any other, shall be punished with death.

Source: For the Colony in Virginea Britannia. Lavves Diuine, Morall and Martiall, &c. (London, 1612), 3-4, 6-7, 12, 14-15.

Mayflower Compact (1620)

Seventy years before the publication of John Locke's Second Treatise of Government, *the English religious dissenters known as the Pilgrims actually lived out his theories of how civil societies are formed. Faced with the terrors of entering an unknown wilderness, these English settlers pledged to form a commonwealth in which the absolute freedom that individuals might enjoy in "nature" would be traded for the safety and security of a community governed by rules and laws.*

IN THE NAME OF GOD, AMEN. We, whose names are underwritten, the Loyal Subjects of our dread Sovereign Lord King *James,* by the Grace of God, of *Great Britain, France,* and *Ireland,* King, *Defender of the Faith,* &c. Having undertaken for the Glory of God, and Advancement of the Christian Faith, and the Honour of our King and Country, a Voyage to plant the first Colony in the northern Parts of *Virginia;* Do by these Presents, solemnly and mutually, in the Presence of God and one another, covenant and combine ourselves together into a civil Body Politick, for our better Ordering and Preservation, and Furtherance of the Ends aforesaid: And by Virtue hereof do enact, constitute, and frame, such just and equal Laws, Ordinances, Acts, Constitutions, and Officers, from time to time, as shall be thought most meet and convenient for the general Good of the Colony; unto which we promise all due Submission and Obedience. IN WITNESS whereof we have hereunto subscribed our names at *Cape-Cod* the eleventh of *November*, in the Reign of our Sovereign Lord King *James*, of *England*, *France*, and *Ireland*, the eighteenth, and of *Scotland* the fifty-fourth, *Anno Domini*; 1620.

Source: Francis Newton Thorpe, ed., *The Federal and State Constitutions, Colonial Charters, and other Organic Laws* (Washington, 1909), 3:1841.

Charter of the Massachusetts Bay Company (1629)

Eager to expand its empire in North America, the English Crown awarded charters to groups of merchants willing to do the difficult and dangerous work of settling the New World. These contracts specified particular land areas to be settled and provided for governmental organization, legal rights, and trade privileges in the new colony. In essence, the New World colonies would provide raw materials for England's burgeoning industries and also serve as a consumer market for finished goods from England. All colonial charters followed this basic model, although the particulars within each individual colony's charter differed. In 1629, a group of Puritans calling themselves the Massachusetts Bay Company secured such a charter for the settlement of their own colony. These settlers had a dual purpose for their venture. In addition to establishing a profitable enterprise, they also were determined to make their colony a model demonstrating the superiority of their religious beliefs, a "city upon a hill," for the world to emulate.

Charles, by the grace of god, King of England, Scotland, France, and Ireland, Defender of the Faith, &c. To ALL to whom these Presents shall come Greeting. *Whereas*, our most Dear and Royal Father, King James, of blessed Memory, by his Highness Letters-patents bearing Date at Westminster the third Day of November, in the eighteenth Year of his Reign, HATH given and granted unto the Council established at Plymouth, in the County of Devon, for the planting, ruling, ordering, and governing of New England in America, and to their Successors and Assigns for ever, all that Part of America, lying and being in Breadth, from Forty Degrees of Northerly Latitude from the Equinoctiall Line, to forty eight Degrees of the said Northerly Latitude inclusively, and in Length, of and within all the Breadth aforesaid, throughout the Maine Lands from Sea to Sea; together also with all the Firm Lands, Soils, Grounds, Havens, Ports, Rivers, Waters, Fishing, Mines, and Minerals, as well Royal Mines of Gold and Silver, as other Mines and Minerals, precious Stones, Quarries, and all and singular other Commodities, Jurisdictions, Royalties, Privileges, Franchises, and Prominences, both within the said Tract of Land upon the Main, and also within the Islands and Seas adjoining....

And our Will and Pleasure is, and We do hereby for Us, our Heirs and Successors, ordain and grant, That from henceforth for ever, there shall be one Governor, one Deputy Governor, and eighteen Assistants of the same Company, to be from time to time constituted, elected and chosen out of the Freemen of the said Company, for the time being, in such Manner and Form as hereafter in these Presents is expressed, which said Officers shall apply themselves to take Care for the best disposing and ordering of the general business and Affairs of, for, and concerning the said Lands and Premises hereby mentioned, to be granted, and the Plantation thereof, and the Government of the People there....

That the Governor, or in his absence, the Deputy Governor of the said Company for the time being, and such of the Assistants and Freemen of the said Company as shall be present, or the greater number of them so assembled, whereof the Governor or Deputy Governor and six of the Assistants at the least to be seven, shall have full Power and authority to choose, nominate, and appoint, such and so many others as they shall think fit, and that shall be willing to accept the same, to be free of the said Company and Body, and them into the same to admit; and to elect and constitute such Officers as they shall think fit and requisite, for the ordering, managing, and dispatching of the Affairs of the said Governor and Company, and their Successors; And to make Laws and Ordinances for the Good and Welfare of the said Company, and for the Government and ordering of the said Lands and Plantation, and the People inhabiting and to inhabit the same, as to them from time to time shall be thought meet, so as such Laws and Ordinances be not contrary or repugnant to the Laws and Statutes of this our Realm of England....

Source: Francis Newton Thorpe, ed., *The Federal and State Constitutions, Colonial Charters, and Other Organic Laws* (Washington, 1909), 3:1852, 1853.

Cases of Conscience Concerning Evil Spirits Personating Men; Witchcrafts, Infallible Proofs of Guilt in such as are Accused with that Crime (1693)

Increase Mather

While the notorious events that shook Salem Village in 1692 represent an anomaly in the legal history of colonial America, the Reverend Increase Mather's statement cautions against injustices occurring due to panic. Mather, an influential Boston minister and president of Harvard College, led a committee of ministers who investigated the conduct of the trials. The document demonstrates the distinctive Puritan understanding of witchcraft as a phenomenon within both the supernatural and the mundane realms. Although its practitioners employed supernatural means in carrying out their malevolent deeds, witchcraft also constituted a particular category of crime and, therefore, was appropriately handled within the legal system, where due process and the rights of the accused must be respected.

Christian Reader,

So Odious and Abominable is the Name of a Witch, to the Civilized, much more the Religious part of Mankind, that it is apt to grow up into a Scandal for any, so much as to enter some sober cautions against the over hasty suspecting, or too precipitant

Judging of the Persons on this account. But certainly, the more execrable the Crime is, the more a critical care is to be used in the exposing of the Names, Liberties, and Lives of men (especially of a Godly Conversation) to the imputation of it. The awful hand of God now upon us, in letting loose of evil Angels among us to perpetrate such horrid Mischiefs; and suffering of Hell's instruments, to do such fearful things as have bin scarce heard of; hath put serious persons into deep Musings, and upon curious Enquiries what is to be done for the detecting and defeating of this tremendous design of the grand Adversary; and, tho' all that fear God are agreed, That no evil is to be done, that Good may come of it; yet hath the Devil obtained not a little of his design, in the divisions of Reuben, about the application of his rule.

That there are Devils and Witches, the Scripture asserts, and experience confirms, That they are common enemies of Mankind, and set upon mischief, is not to be doubted: That the Devil can (by Divine Permission) and often doth vex men in Body and Estate, without the Instrumentality of Witches, is undeniable: That he often hath, and delights to have the Concurrence of Witches, and their consent in harming men, is consonant to his native Malice to Man, and too Lamentably exemplified: That Witches, when detected or convinced, ought to be exterminated and cut off, we have God's warrant for; Exod. 22.18. Only the same God who hath said, thou shalt not suffer a Witch to live; hath also said, at the Mouth of two Witnesses, or three Witnesses shall be that is worthy of Death, be put to Death: But at the Mouth of one Witness, he shall not be put to Death. Deut. 17.6. Much debate is made about what is sufficient Conviction, and some have (in their Zeal) supposed that a less clear evidence ought to pass in this than in other cases, supposing that else it will be hard (if possible) to bring such to Condign Punishment, by reason of the close conveyances that there are between the Devil and Witches; but this is a very dangerous, and unjustifiable tenet. Men serve God in doing their Duty: he never intended that all persons guilty of Capital Crimes should be discovered and punished by men in this Life, though they be never so curious in searching after Iniquity. It is therefore exceeding necessary that in such a day as this, men be informed what is Evidence, and what is not. It concerns men in point of Charity; for, tho' the most shining Professor may be secretly a most abominable Sinner, yet till he be detected, our Charity is bound to Judge according to what appears: and notwithstanding that a clear evidence must determine a case; yet presumptions must be weighed against presumptions, and Charity is not to be forgone as long as it hath the most preponderance on its side. And it is of no less necessity in point of Justice; there are not only Testimonies required by God, which are to be Credited according to the rules given in his Word referring to witnesses: But there is also an Evidence supposed to be in the Testimony, which is thoroughly to be weighed, and if it do not infallibly prove the Crime against the person accused, it ought not to determine him guilty of it; for so a righteous Man may be Condemned unjustly. In the case of Witchcrafts we know that the Devil is the immediate Agent in the Mischief done, the consent or compact of the Witch is the thing to be Demonstrated.

Among many Arguments to evince this, that which is most under present debate, is that which refers to something vulgarly, called Spectre Evidence, and a certain sort of Ordeal or trial by the sight and touch. The principal Plea to justify the convictive Evidence in these, is fetcht from the Consideration of the Wisdom and Righteousness of God in Governing the World, which they suppose would fail, if such things were permitted to befal an innocent person: but it is certain, that too resolute conclusions drawn from hence, are bold usurpations upon spotless Sovereignty: and tho' some things, if suffered to be common, would subvert this Government, and disband, yea ruine Humane Society; yet God doth sometimes suffer such things to evene, that we may thereby know how much we are beholden to him, for that restraint which he lays upon the Infernal Spirits, who would else reduce a World into a Chaos. That the Resolutions of such Cases as these is proper for the Servants of Christ in the Ministry cannot be denied; The reasonableness of doing it now, will be Justified by the Consideration of the necessity there is at this time of a right Information of Mens Judgments about these things, and the danger of their being misinformed.

The Reverend, Learned, and Judicious Author of the ensuing Cases, is too well known to need our Commendation: all that we are concerned in, is to assert our hearty Consent to, and Concurrence with the substance of what is contained in the following Discourse: and, with our hearty Request to God, that he would discover the depths of this Hellish Design; direct in the whole management of this Affair; prevent the taking any wrong steps in this dark way; and that he would in particular Bless these faithful Endeavors of his Servant to that end, we Commend it and you to His Divine Benediction.

Source: Increase Mather, *Cases of Conscience Concerning Evil Spirits Personating Men; Witchcrafts, Infallible Proofs of Guilt in such As are Accused with that Crime* (Boston, 1693).

Slave Statutes (1669 and 1680)

The vast labor force required to make the colonies succeed drew from free labor, indentured servitude, apprenticeships, and the child "placing-out" system, and, of course, slavery. Unfortunately, because the vast majority of the colonial work-force was illiterate, we have little evidence today to illuminate the experiences of these varying groups of workers. What is clear, however, is that race took on an increasing significance. After 1660 slavery began to be written into colonial statute laws, with the effect that the status of African slaves became increasingly distinguished from that of English servants. The new slave codes placed tight restrictions on the behavior of individual slaves and allowed a high degree of discretionary authority over them to their white masters.

ACT I.
[October 1669]

An act about the casuall killing of slaves.

Whereas the only law in force for the punishment of refractory servants resisting their master, mistris or overseer cannot be inflicted upon negroes, nor the obstinacy of many of them by other then violent meanes supprest, *Be it enacted and declared by this grand assembly* if any slave resist his master (or other by his masters order correcting him) and by the extremity of the correction should chance to die, that his death shall not be accompted felony, but the master (or that other person appointed by the master to punish him) be acquit from molestation, since it cannot be presumed that prepensed malice (which alone makes murther felony) should induce any man to destroy his owne estate.

ACT X.
[June 1680]

An act for preventing Negroes Insurrections.

Whereas the frequent meeting of considerable numbers of negroe slaves under pretence of feasts and burialls is judged of dangerous consequence; for prevention whereof for the future, *Bee it enacted by the kings most excellent majestie by and with the consent of the generall assembly and it is hereby enacted the authority aforesaid,* that from and after the publication of this law, it shall not be lawfull for any negroe or other slave to carry or arme himselfe with any club, staffe, gunn, sword or any other weapon of defence or offence, nor to goe or depart from of his masters ground without a certificate from his master, mistris or overseer, and such permission not to be granted but upon perticuler and necessary occasions; and every negroe or slave soe offending not haveing a certificate as aforesaid shalbe sent to the next constable, who is hereby enjoyned and required to give the said negroe twenty lashes on his bare back welllayd on, and soe sent home to his said master, mistris or overseer. *And it is further enacted by the authority aforesaid* that if any negroe or other slave shall presume to lift up his hand in opposition against any christian, shall for every such offence, upon due proofe made thereof by the oath of the party before a magistrate, have and receive thirty lashes on his bare back well laid on. *And it is hereby further enacted by the authority aforesaid* that if any negroe or other slave shall absent himself from his masters service and lye hid and lurking in obscure places, comitting injuries to the inhabitants, and shall resist any person or persons that shalby any lawfull authority be imployed to apprehend and take the said negroe, that then in case of such resistance, it shalbe lawfull for such person or persons to kill the said negroe or slave soe lying out and resisting, and that this law be once every six months published at the respective county courts and parish churches within this colony.

Source: William Waller Hening, *The Statutes at Large: Being a Collection of the Laws of Virginia* (New York, 1823), 2:270, 481–482.

A Brief Narrative of the Case and Trial of John Peter Zenger, Printer of the New-York *Weekly Journal* (1735)

In 1735 John Peter Zenger was tried for printing seditious statements against the governor of New York Province, but the jury acquitted him. The arguments made by Zenger's attorney, Andrew Hamilton, clearly reflect the fact that by the mid-eighteenth century the differing social and economic contexts of England and the North American colonies had produced a divergence of thinking about the common law. The state's authority to punish libel against the government derived from the English Common Law tenet that such speech might incite a riot and threaten the public safety. Under the Common Law truth was no defense – in fact, truth actually aggravated the crime. The Common Law reasoned that inflammatory true statements might stir up a riot more than obviously false ones. But the colonial jury favored Hamilton's defense that the state could not punish his client for his criticisms of the governor because the statements were true. The jury, in fact, nullified the law.

Mr. Attorney....The Case before the Court is, whether Mr. *Zenger* is guilty of Libelling His Excellency the Governor of *New York*, and indeed the whole Administration of the Government? Mr. *Hamilton* has confessed the Printing and Publishing, and I think nothing is plainer, than that the Words in the Information are *scandalous, and tend to sedition, and to disquiet the Minds of the People of this Province.* And if such Papers are not Libels, I think it may be said, there can be no such Thing as a Libel.

Mr. Hamilton. May it please Your Honour; I cannot agree with Mr. Attorney: For tho' I freely acknowledge, that there are such

Things as Libels, yet I must insist at the same Time, that what my Client is charged with, is not a Libel; and I observed just now, that Mr. Attorney in defining a Libel, made use of the Words, *scandalous, seditious, and tend to disquiet the People*; but (whether with Design or not I will not say) he omitted the Word *false*.

Mr. Attorney. I think I did not omit the Word *false*: But it has been said already, that it may be Libel, notwithstanding it may be true.

Mr. Hamilton. In this I must still differ with Mr. Attorney; for I depend upon it, we are to be tried upon this Information now before the Court and Jury, and to which we have pleaded *Not Guilty*, and by it we are charged....To shew the Court that I am in good Earnest, and to save the Court's Time, and Mr. Attorney's Trouble, I will agree, that if he can prove the Facts charged upon us, to be *false*, I'll own them to be *scandalous, seditious*, and *a Libel*. So the Work seems now to be pretty much shortened, and Mr. Attorney has now only to prove the Words *false*, in order to make us Guilty....

Mr. Chief. Justice. Mr. *Hamilton*, the Court is of Opinion, you ought not to be permitted to prove the Facts in the Papers: These are the Words of the Book, *"It is far from being a Justification of a Libel, that the Contents thereof are true, or that the Person upon whom it is made, had a bad Reputation, since the greater Appearance there is of truth in any malicious Invective, so much the more provoking it is."*

Mr. Hamilton. These are Star Chamber Cases, and I was in hopes, that Practice had been dead with the Court.

Mr. Ch. Just. Mr. *Hamilton*, the Court have delivered their Opinion, and we expect you will use us with good Manners; you are not to be permitted to argue against the Opinion of the Court.

Mr. Hamilton. With Submission, I have seen the Practice in very great Courts, and never heard it deemed unmannerly to—

Mr. Ch. Just. After the Court have declared their Opinion, it is not good Manners to insist upon a Point, in which you are overruled.

Mr. Hamilton. I will say no more at this Time; the Court I see is against us in this Point; and that I hope I may be allowed to say.

Mr. Ch. Just. Use the Court with Good Manners, and you shall be allowed all the Liberty you can reasonably desire.

Mr. Hamilton. I thank Your Honour. Then Gentlemen of the Jury, it is to you we must now appeal, for Witnesses, to the Truth of the Facts we have offered, and are denied the Liberty to prove; ...according to my Brief, the Facts which we offer to prove were not committed in a Corner; they are notoriously known to be true; and therefore in your Justice lies our Safety....

Mr. Ch. Just. No, Mr. *Hamilton*; the Jury may find that *Zenger* printed and published those Papers, and leave it to the Court to judge whether they are libellous....

Mr. Hamilton. I know, may it please Your Honour, the Jury may do so; but I do likewise know, they may do otherwise. I know they have the Right beyond all Dispute, to determine both the Law and the Fact, and where they do not doubt of the Law, they ought to do so. This of leaving it to the Judgment of the Court, *whether the Words are libellous or not*, in Effect renders Juries useless (to say no worse) in many Cases.... It is true in Times past it was a Crime to speak Truth, and in that terrible Court of Star Chamber, many worthy and brave Men suffered for so doing; and yet even in that Court, and in those bad Times, a great and good Man durst say, what I hope will not be taken amiss of me to say in this Place, to wit, *The Practice of Informations for Libels is a Sword in the Hands of a wicked King, and an errant Coward, to cut down and destroy the innocent; the one cannot, because of his High Station, and the other dares not, because of his Want of Courage, revenge himself in another Manner.*

Mr. Attorney. Pray Mr. *Hamilton*, have a Care what you say, don't go too far neither, I don't like those Liberties....

Mr. Hamilton... May it please Your Honour, I was saying, That notwithstanding all the Duty and Reverence claimed by Mr. Attorney to Men in Authority, they are not exempt from observing the Rules of common Justice, either in their private or publick Capacities....

[T]he Question before the Court and you, Gentlemen of the Jury, is not of small nor private Concern, it is not the Cause of a poor Printer, nor of *New-York* alone, which you are now trying: No! It may in its Consequence, affect every Freeman that lives under a British Government on the Main of *America*. It is the best Cause. It is the Cause of Liberty....

Mr. Ch. Just. Gentlemen of the Jury. The great Pains Mr. *Hamilton* has taken, to shew how little Regard Juries are to Pay to Opinion of the Judges; and his insisting so much upon the Conduct of some Judges in Trials of this kind; is done no doubt, with a Design that you should take but very little Notice of what I may say upon this Occasion. I shall therefore only observe to you that, as the Facts or Words in the Information are confessed: The only Thing that can come in Question before you is, whether the Words as set forth in the Information, makes a Libel. And that is a Matter of Law, no doubt, and which you may leave to the Court....

The Jury withdrew, and in a small Time returned, and being asked by the Clerk, Whether they were agreed of their Verdict, and whether *John Peter Zenger* was guilty of Printing and Publishing the Libels in the Information mentioned? They answered by *Thomas Hunt*, their Foreman, *Not Guilty*. Upon which there were three Huzzas in the Hall which was crowded with People, and the next Day I was discharged from my Imprisonment.

Source: John Peter Zenger, *A Brief Narrative of the Case and Tryal of John Peter Zenger, Printer of the New-York* Weekly Journal (New York, 1736), 21–22, 25, 27, 28, 39, 40.

Blackstone on Married Women's Status (1765)

As we saw in Chapter 1, William Blackstone's Commentaries on the Laws of England *served as the definitive source on the English Common Law. In this excerpt, Blackstone explains the notion of "coverture" in which married women's legal status was "covered" by that of their husbands; they had no independent identity in the eyes of the law. The legal status of* feme covert *(literally "covered woman") conveyed a complex set of restrictions, obligations, and protections to married women. These Common-Law precepts applied to English women of all social and economic classes, living in England or living in the North American colonies.*

By marriage, the husband and wife are one person in law: that is, the very being or legal existence of the woman is suspended during the marriage, or at least is incorporated and consolidated into that of the husband: under whose wing, protection, and *cover*, she performs every thing; and is therefore called in our law-french a *feme-covert*; is said to be *covert-baron*, or under the protection and influence of her husband, her *baron*, or lord; and her condition during her marriage is called her *coverture*. Upon this principle, of an union of person in husband and wife, depend almost all the legal rights, duties, and disabilities, that either of them acquire by the marriage. I speak not at present of the rights of property, but of such as are merely *personal*. For this reason, a man cannot grant anything to his wife, or enter into covenant with her: for the grant would be to suppose her separate existence; and to covenant with her, would be only to covenant with himself: and therefore it is also generally true, that all compacts made between husband and wife, when single, are voided by the intermarriage. A woman indeed may be attorney for her husband; for that implies no separation from, but is rather a representation of, her lord. And a husband may also bequeath any thing to his wife by will; for that cannot take effect til the coverture is determined by his death. The husband is bound to provide his wife with necessaries by law, as much as himself; and if she contracts debts for them, he is obliged to pay them: but for any thing besides necessities, he is not chargeable. Also if a wife elopes, and lives with another man, the husband is not chargeable even for necessaries; at least if the person, who furnishes them, is sufficiently apprized of her elopement. If the wife be indebted before marriage, the husband is bound afterwards to pay the debt; for he has adopted her and her circumstances together. If the wife be injured in her person or her property, she can bring no action for redress without her husband's concurrence, and in his name, as well as her own: neither can she be sued, without making the husband a defendant. There is indeed one case where the wife shall sue and be sued as a feme sole, viz. where the husband has abjured the realm, or is banished: for then he is dead in the law; and, the husband being thus disabled to sue for or defend the wife, it would be most unreasonable if she had no remedy, or could make no defense at all. In criminal prosecutions, it is true, the wife may be indicted and punished separately; for the union is only a civil union. But, in trials of any sort, they are not allowed to be evidence for, or against, each other: partly because it is impossible that their testimony should be indifferent; but principally because of the union of person.... But where the offence is directly against the person of the wife, this rule has been usually dispensed with: and therefore, by statute 3 Hen. VII. c. 2, in case a woman be forcibly taken away, and married, she may be a witness against such her husband, in order to convict him of a felony. For in this case she can with no propriety be reckoned his wife; because a main ingredient, her consent, was wanting to the contract: and also there is another maxim of law, that no man shall take advantage of his own wrong; which the ravisher here would do, if by forcibly marrying a woman, he could prevent her from being a witness, who is perhaps the only witness, to that very fact....

But, though our law in general considers man and wife as one person, yet there are some instances in which she is separately considered; as inferior to him, and acting by his compulsion. And therefore all deeds executed, and acts done, by her, during her coverture, are void, or at least voidable; except it be a fine, or the like matter of record, in which case she must be solely and secretly examined, to learn if her act be voluntary. She cannot by will devise lands to her husband, unless under special circumstances; for at the time of making it she is supposed to be under his coercion. And in some felonies, and other inferior crimes, committed by her, through constraint of her husband, the law excludes her: but this extends not to treason or murder.

The husband also (by the old law) might give his wife moderate correction. For, as he is to answer for her misbehavior, the law thought it reasonable to intrust him with this power of restraining her, by domestic chastisement, in the same moderation that a man is allowed to correct his servants or children; for whom the master or parent is also liable in some cases to answer. But this power of correction was confined within reasonable bounds; and the husband was prohibited to use violence to his wife....The civil law gave the husband the same, or a larger, authority over his wife.... But, with us, in the politer reign of Charles the second, this power of correction began to be doubted: and a wife may now have the security of the peace against her husband; or, in return, a husband against his wife. Yet the lower rank of people, who were always fond of the old common law, still claim and exert their antient privilege: and the courts of law will still permit a husband to restrain a wife of her liberty, in case of any gross misbehavior.

Source: William Blackstone, *Commentaries on the Laws of England* (Oxford, 1765), 1:430–433.

3.

The American Revolution

The long period of "salutary neglect" in which the American colonies grew and prospered began to unravel in 1754 when Great Britain entered the Seven Years War to protect its imperial interests. Heavily in debt and anxious to increase the efficiency of administering its expanding empire, Parliament's attempts to exert more control over the North American colonies were met with stiff resistance. Over time, many Americans had come to view their relationship with England as a kind of federation in which Parliament and the Crown directed "external" matters such as foreign policy and war while the individual legislatures remained sovereign to conduct "internal" affairs in the colonies. Thus they reacted with alarm to Parliament's unprecedented reach across the Atlantic. English men and women in the colonies especially resented their lack of representation in a distant legislature that imposed taxation measures on them for the first time. A small but vocal minority invoked the theories of natural rights and social contract to argue that the government in England was failing to protect their interests. The American colonists began a journey that would take them from being loyal subjects of the Crown to participants in a long and bloody war for their independence.

Virginia Stamp Act Resolutions (1765)

With the close of the Seven Years War, Parliament struggled to pay off the enormous debt incurred in that struggle. Members of Parliament needed to enact a taxation policy that distributed the costs equitably among all English citizens, those in the colonies as well as in England itself. Parliament passed a Sugar Act in 1764 and a Stamp Act the following year.

Colonists protested the new taxes. In Virginia, the legislature passed resolutions that reaffirmed the colonies' loyalty to England. The colonists proclaimed their loyalty as "liege People." Liege means loyal. The colonists, though, also said that as loyal English citizens they had English constitutional rights. The English Constitution, though unwritten, protected the rights of English citizens from taxation without representation.

Mr. *Attorney*, from the Committee of the whole House, reported, according to Order, that the Committee had considered of the Steps necessary to be taken in Consequence of the Resolutions of the House of Commons of *Great Britain* relative to the charging Stamp Duties in the colonies and Plantations in *America*, that they had come to several Resolutions thereon; which he read in his Place, and then delivered in at the Table, where they were again twice read, and agreed to by the House, and some Amendments, and are as follow:

Resolved, That the first Adventurers and Settlers of this his Majesty's Colony and Dominion of *Virginia* brought with them, and transmitted to their Posterity, and all other his Majesty's Subjects since inhabiting in this his Majesty's said Colony, all the Liberties, Privileges, Franchises, and Immunities, that have at any Time been held, enjoyed, possessed, by the people of *Great Britain.*

Resolved, That by two royal Charters, granted by King *James* the First, the Colonists aforesaid are declared entitled to all Liberties, Privileges, and Immunities of Denizens and natural Subjects, to all Intents and Purposes, as if they had been abiding and born within the Realm of *England.*

Resolved, That the Taxation of the People by themselves, or by Persons chosen by themselves to represent them, who can only know what Taxes the People are able to bear, or the eafiest

Method of raising them, and must themselves be affected by every Tax laid on the People, is the only Security against a burthensome Taxation, and the distinguishing Characteristick of *British* Freedom, without which the ancient Constitution cannot exist.

Resolved, That his Majesty's liege People of this his most ancient and loyal Colony have without Interruption enjoyed the inestimable Right of being governed by such Laws, respecting their internal Polity and Taxation, as are derived from their own Consent, with the Approbation of their Sovereign, or his Substitute; and that the fame hath never been forfeited or yielded up, but hath been constantly recognized by the Kings and People of *Great Britain.*

Source: John Pendleton Kennedy, ed., *Journals of the House of Burgesses of Virginia, 1761-65*, (Richmond, 1907), 360.

Parliamentary Debate on Taxation (1766)

The colonists were not without friends in Parliament. Members of Parliament arguing on behalf of the colonial position presented the English Constitution as fixed while their opponents understood it as flexible, capable of growth. Americans would later have similar arguments about their own Constitution.

March 17, 1766.

As to the right of taxation, the gentlemen who opposed it, produced many learned authorities from Locke, Selden, Harrington, and Puffendorf, shewing 'that the very foundation and ultimate point in view of all government, is the good of the society.'

That by going up to Magna Charta, and referring to the several writs upon record, issued out for the purpose of raising taxes for the crown, and for sending representatives to parliament, as well as from the Bill of Rights, it appears throughout the whole history of our constitution, that no British subject can be taxed but ...of himself, or his own representative; and this is that first and general right as British subjects, with which the first inhabitants of the colonies emigrated....

That many people carry the idea of a parliament too far, in supposing a parliament can do every thing; but that is not true, and if it were, it is not right constitutionally: for then there might be an arbitrary power in a parliament, as well as in one man. — There are many things a parliament cannot do....It cannot take any man's property, even that of the meanest cottager...without his being heard....

These arguments were answered with great force of reason, and knowledge of the constitution, from the other side. They observed it was necessary to clear away from the question, all that mass of dissertation and learning, displayed in arguments which have been brought from speculative men, who have written upon the subject of government. That the refinements upon that subject, and arguments of natural lawyers, as Locke, Selden, Puffendorf, and others, are little to the purpose in a question of constitutional law. That it is absurd to apply records from the earliest times to our present constitution; because the constitution is not the same: and nobody knows what it was at some of the times that are quoted: that there are things even in Magna Charta which are not constitution now, and that those records are no proofs of our constitution as it now is.

The constitution of this country has been always in a moving state, either gaining or losing something....

Source: The Parliamentary History of England from the Earliest Period to the Year 1803 (London, 1813), 16:194–197.

Letters from a Pennsylvania Farmer to the Inhabitants of the British Colonies (1768)

John Dickinson

In 1767, Parliament again tried to raise money and at the same time improve the efficiency of administering the colonies in a series of measures called the Townshend Duties. Like their precedent, the Stamp Act, the new measures provoked petitions of protest, the boycott of British goods, and mob action in the colonies.

A series of pamphlets written by John Dickinson, a highly respected lawyer in Philadelphia, proved to be extremely influential in shaping the discourse of colonial protest. A political moderate, Dickinson avoided the hyperbole of other protest literature circulating at that time and instead presented an argument rooted in the English traditions of constitutionalism. While Parliament did retain the authority to enact measures promoting the general welfare of the empire, Dickinson insisted that Parliament had no constitutional power to tax the colonies for the purpose of raising revenue alone. Dickinson's rhetoric demonstrates the cracks that had begun to appear in the federalist model under which England governed its North American colonies. In 1770, Parliament repealed the Townshend Duties.

LETTER II.

My dear Countrymen,

...The parliament unquestionably possesses a legal authority to *regulate* the trade of *Great-Britain*, and all its colonies. Such an authority is essential to the relation between a mother country and its colonies; and necessary for the common good of all. He, who considers these provinces as states distinct from the *British Empire*, has very slender notions of *justice* or of their *interests*. We are but parts of a *whole*; and therefore there must exist a power somewhere, to preside, and preserve the connection in due order. This power is lodged in the parliament; and we are as much dependent on *Great-Britain*, as a perfectly free people can be on another.

I have looked over *every statute* relating to these colonies, from their first settlement to this time; and I find every one of them founded on this principle, till the *Stamp Act* administration. *All before* are calculated to regulate trade, and preserve or promote a mutually beneficial intercourse between the several constituent parts of the empire; and though many of them imposed duties on trade, yet those duties were always imposed *with design* to restrain the commerce of one part, that was injurious to another, and thus to promote the general welfare. The raising a revenue thereby was never intended. Thus, the king, by his judges in his courts of justice, imposes fines which all together amount to a very considerable sum, and contribute to the support of government: but this is merely a consequence arising from restrictions, which only meant to keep peace, and prevent confusion; and surely a man would argue very loosely, who should conclude from hence, that the King has a right to levy money in general upon his subjects; Never did the *British* parliament, till the period above mentioned, think of imposing duties in *America*, FOR THE PURPOSE OF RAISING A REVENUE....

A few months after came the Stamp-Act, which reciting this, proceeds in the same strange mode of expression, thus— "And whereas it is just and necessary, that provision be MADE FOR RAISING A FURTHER REVENUE WITHIN YOUR MAJESTY'S DOMINIONS IN AMERICA, *towards defraying the said experiences,* we your Majesty's most dutiful and loyal subjects, the COMMONS OF GREAT-BRITAIN, &C. GIVE AND GRANT," &c. as before....

Here we may observe an authority *expressly* claimed to impose duties on these colonies; not for the regulation of trade; not for the preservation or promotion of a mutually beneficial intercourse between the several constituent parts of the empire, heretofore the *sole objects* of parliamentary institutions; *but for the single purpose of levying money upon us.*

This I call an innovation; and a most dangerous innovation....

LETTER IV.

...Whenever we speak of "taxes" among *Englishmen,* let us therefore speak of them with reference to the *principles* on which, and the *intentions* with which they have been established. This will give certainty to our expression, and safety to our conduct: But if, when we have in view the liberty of these colonies, we proceed in any other course, we pursue a *Juno* indeed, but shall only catch a cloud....

A "TAX" means an imposition to raise money. Such persons therefore as speak of *internal* and *external* "TAXES," I pray may pardon me, if I object to that expression, as applied to the privileges and interests of these colonies. There may be *internal* and *external* IMPOSITIONS, founded on *different principles,* every "tax" being an imposition, tho' every imposition is not a "tax." But *all taxes* are founded on the *same principles*; and have the *same tendency*.

External impositions for the regulation of our trade, do not "grant to his Majesty *the property of the colonies*." They only *prevent the colonies acquiring property*, in things not necessary, in a manner judged to be injurious to the welfare of the whole empire. But the last statute respecting us "grants to his Majesty *the property of these colonies*," by laying duties on manufactures of *Great-Britain* which they MUST take, and which he settled them, in order that they SHOULD take.

What *tax* can be more *internal* than this? Here is money drawn, *without their consent*, from a society, who have constantly enjoyed a constitutional mode of raising all money among themselves. The payment of their *tax* they have no possible method of avoiding; as they cannot do without the commodities on which it is laid, and they cannot manufacture these commodities themselves. Besides, if this unhappy country should be so lucky as to elude this act, by getting parchment enough, to use in the place of paper, or reviving the antient method of writing on wax and bark, and by inventing something to serve instead of glass, her ingenuity would stand her in little stead; for then the parliament would have nothing to do but to prohibit manufactures, or to lay a tax on *hats* and *woollen cloths*, which they have already prohibited the colonies *from supplying each other with*; or on instruments, and tools of *steel* and *iron*, which they have prohibited the provincials *from manufacturing at all*: And then, what little gold and silver they have, must be torn from their hands, or they will not be able, in a short time, to get an ax, for cutting their firewood, nor a plough for raising their food....

Source: Paul Leicester Ford, ed., *The Writings of John Dickinson* (Philadelphia, 1895), 1:312-322, 330, 332–334.

Common Sense (1776)

Thomas Paine

Thomas Paine had only lived in the colonies for one year when his revolutionary pamphlet burst upon the colonial scene in early 1776. More than 100,000 copies sold within three months. Shifting the focus of the debate from Parliament's authority to the very existence of the monarchy, Paine took the American colonists to the edge of rebellion. But in advocating the overthrow of the king, Paine also argued for his replacement not by another monarch, but instead by a republican form of government sustained solely by the will of the governed. It was a breathlessly bold proposal, and yet within the year, colonial leaders meeting in Philadelphia took the plunge.

Some writers have so confounded society with government, as to leave little or distinction between them; whereas they are not only different, but have different origins. Society is produced by our wants, and government by our wickedness; the former promotes our wants, and government by our wickedness; the former promotes our happiness *positively* by uniting our affections, the later *negatively* by restraining our vices. The one encourages intercourse, the other creates distinctions. The first is a patron, the last a punisher.

Society in every state is a blessing, but government in its best state is but a necessary evil; in its worst state an intolerable one; for when we suffer, or are exposed to the same miseries *by a government*, which we might expect in a country *without government*, our calamity is heightened by reflecting that we furnish the means by which we suffer. Government, like dress, is the badge of lost innocence; the palaces of kings are built on the ruins of the bowers of paradise. For were the impulses of conscience clear, uniform, and irresistibly obeyed, man would need no other lawgiver; but that not being the case, he finds it necessary to surrender up a part of his property to furnish means for the protection of the rest; and this he is induced to do by the same prudence which in every other case advises him out of two evils to choose the least. *Therefore*, security being the true design and end of government, it unanswerably follows that whatever *form* thereof appears most likely to ensure it to us, with the least expence and greatest benefit, is preferable to all others....

Here, then is the origin of and rise of government; namely, a mode rendered necessary by the inability of moral virtue to govern the world; here too is the design and end of government, viz., freedom and security. And however our eyes may be dazzled with show, or our ears deceived by sound; however prejudice may warp our wills, or interest darken our understanding, the simple voice of nature and of reason will say, it is right.

I draw my idea of the form of government from a principle, in nature, which no art can overturn, viz. that the more simple anything is, the less liable it is to be disordered; and the easier repaired when disordered; and with this maxim in view, I offer a few remarks on the so much boasted constitution of England. That is was noble for the dark and slavish times in which it was erected, is granted. When the world was over run with tyranny the least remove therefrom was a glorious rescue. But that it is imperfect, subject to convulsions, and incapable of producing what it seems to promise, is easily demonstrated.

Absolute governments (tho' the disgrace of human nature) have this advantage with them, that they are simple; if the people suffer, they know the head from which their suffering springs, know likewise the remedy, and are not bewildered by a variety of causes and cures. But the constitution of England is so exceedingly complex, that the nation may suffer for years together without being able to discover in which part the fault lies, some will say in one and some in another, and every political physician will advise a different medicine.

I know it is difficult to get over local or long standing prejudices, yet if we will suffer ourselves to examine the component parts of the English constitution, we shall find them to be the base remains of two ancient tyrannies, compounded with some new republican materials.

First. —The remains of monarchial tyranny in the person of the king.

Secondly. — The remains of aristocratical tyranny in the persons of the peers.

Thirdly. — The new republican materials, in the persons of the commons, on whose virtue depends the freedom of England.

The two first, be being hereditary, are independent of the people; wherefore in a *constitutional* sense they contribute nothing toward the freedom of the state.

To say that the constitution of England in a *union* of three powers reciprocally *checking* each other, is farcical, either the words have no meaning, or they are flat contradictions.

To say that the commons is a check upon the king, presupposes two things:

First. —That the king is not to be trusted without being looked after, or in other words, that a thirst for absolute power is the natural disease of monarchy.

Secondly. — That the commons, by being appointed for that purpose, are either wiser or more worthy of confidence than the crown.

But as the same constitution which gives the commons a power to check the king by withholding the supplies, gives afterwards the king a power to check the commons, by empowering him to reject their other bills; it again supposes that the king is wiser than those whom it has already supposed to be wiser than him. A mere absurdity!

There is something exceedingly ridiculous in the composition of monarchy; it first excludes a man from the means of information, yet empowers him to act in cases where the highest judgment is required. The state of a king shuts him from the world, yet the business of a king requires him to know it thoroughly; wherefore the different parts, by unnaturally opposing and destroying each other, prove the whole character to be absurd and useless.

Some writers have explained the English constitution thus; the king, say they, is one, the people another; the peers are a house in behalf of the king; the commons in behalf of the people; but this hath all the distinctions of a house divided against itself; and though the expressions be pleasantly arranged, yet when examined, they appear idle and ambiguous; and it will always happen, that the nicest construction that words of capable of, when applied to the description of something which either cannot exist, or is too incomprehensible to be within the compass of description, will be words of sound only, and though they may amuse the ear, they cannot inform the mind, for this explanation includes a previous question, viz., *How came the king by a power which the people are afraid to trust, and always obliged to check.* Such a power could not be the gift of a wise people, neither can any power, *which needs checking*, be from God; yet the provision, which the constitution makes, supposes such a power to exist....

That the crown is this overbearing part in the English constitution, needs not be mentioned, and that it derives it whole consequence merely from being the giver of places and pensions, is self-evident, wherefore, though we have been wise enough to shut and lock a door against absolute monarchy, we at the same time have been foolish enough to put the crown in possession of the key.

The prejudice of Englishmen, in favour of their own government by king, lords and commons, arises as much or more from national pride than reason. Individuals are undoubtedly safer in England than in some other countries, but the *will* of the king is as much the *law* of the land in Britain as in France, with this difference, that instead of proceeding directly from his mouth, it is handed to the people under the more formidable shape of an act of parliament. For the fate of Charles the First hath only made kings more subtle — not more just.

Wherefore, laying aside all national pride and prejudice in favour of modes and forms, the plain truth is, that *it is wholly owing to the constitution of the people, and not to the constitution of the government*, that the crown is not as oppressive in England as in Turkey....

I have heard it asserted by some, that as America hath flourished under her former connection with Great-Britain, that the same connection is necessary towards her future happiness, and will always have the same effect. Nothing can be more fallacious than this kind of argument. We may as well assert that because a child has thrived upon milk, that it is never to have meat, or that the first twenty years of our lives is to become a precedent for the next twenty. But even this is admitting more than is true, for I answer roundly, that America would have flourished as much, and probably much more, had no European power had any thing to do with her. The commerce, by which she hath enriched herself, are the necessaries of life, and will always have a market while eating is the custom of Europe....

But the injuries and disadvantages we sustain by that connection, are without number; and our duty to mankind at large, as well as to ourselves, instruct us to renounce the alliance: Because, any submission to, or dependence on Great-Britain, tends directly to involve this continent in European wars and quarrels; and sets us at variance with nations, who would otherwise seek our friendship, and against whom, we have neither anger nor complaint. As Europe is our market for trade, we ought to form no partial connection with any part of it. It is the true interest of America to steer clear of European contentions, which she never can do, while by her dependence on Britain, she is made the make-weight of the scale of British politics....

Source: Thomas Paine, *Common Sense ; Addressed to the Inhabitants of America* (n.p., 1776), iii, v, vi, vii, 15, 17.

Declaration of Independence (1776)

The Declaration of Independence represents the climax of England's imperial crisis in the mid-eighteenth century. Thomas Jefferson's soaring rhetoric grounded the colonists' cause in the political traditions of natural rights theory while at the same time casting their revolutionary actions in universal truths.

In Congress, July 4, 1776

The unanimous Declaration of the thirteen united States of America

When in the Course of human events, it becomes necessary for one people to dissolve the political bands which have connected them with another, and to assume among the powers of the earth, the separate and equal station to which the Laws of Nature and of Nature's God entitle them, a decent respect to the opinions of mankind requires that they should declare the causes which impel them to the separation.

We hold these truths to be self-evident, that all men are created equal, that they are endowed by their Creator with certain unalienable Rights, that among these are Life, Liberty and the pursuit of Happiness. That to secure these rights, Governments are instituted among Men, deriving their just powers from the consent of the governed, That whenever any Form of Government becomes destructive of these ends, it is the Right of the People to alter or to abolish it, and to institute new Government, laying its foundation on such principles and organizing its powers in such form, as to them shall seem most likely to effect their Safety and Happiness. Prudence, indeed, will dictate that Governments long established should not be changed for light and transient causes; and accordingly all experience hath shown, that mankind are more disposed to suffer, while evils are sufferable, than to right themselves by abolishing the forms to which they are accustomed. But when a long train of abuses and usurpations, pursuing invariably the same Object evinces a design to reduce them under absolute Despotism, it is their right, it is their duty, to throw off such Government, and to provide new Guards for their future security. —Such has been the patient sufferance of these Colonies; and such is now the necessity which constrains them to alter their former Systems of Government. The history of the present King of Great Britain is a history of repeated injuries and usurpations, all having in direct object the establishment of an absolute Tyranny over these States. To prove this, let Facts be submitted to a candid world.

He has refused his Assent to Laws, the most wholesome and necessary for the public good.

He has forbidden his Governors to pass Laws of immediate and pressing importance, unless suspended in their operation till his Assent should be obtained; and when so suspended, he has utterly neglected to attend to them.

He has refused to pass other Laws for the accommodation of large districts of people, unless those people would relinquish the right of Representation in the Legislature, a right inestimable to them and formidable to tyrants only.

He has called together legislative bodies at places unusual, uncomfortable, and distant from the depository of their Public Records, for the sole purpose of fatiguing them into compliance with his measures.

He has dissolved Representative Houses repeatedly, for opposing with manly firmness his invasions on the rights of the people.

He has refused for a long time, after such dissolutions, to cause others to be elected; whereby the Legislative Powers, incapable of Annihilation, have returned to the People at large for their exercise; the State remaining in the mean time exposed to all the dangers of invasion from without, and convulsions within.

He has endeavoured to prevent the population of these States; for that purpose obstructing the Laws for Naturalization of Foreigners; refusing to pass others to encourage their migrations hither, and raising the conditions of new Appropriations of Lands.

He has obstructed the Administration of Justice, by refusing his Assent to Laws for establishing Judiciary Powers.

He has made Judges dependent on his Will alone, for the tenure of their offices, and the amount and payment of their salaries.

He has erected a multitude of New Offices, and sent hither swarms of Officers to harrass our people, and eat out their substance.

He has kept among us, in times of peace, Standing Armies without the Consent of our legislatures.

He has affected to render the Military independent of and superior to the Civil Power.

He has combined with others to subject us to a jurisdiction foreign to our constitution, and unacknowledged by our laws; giving his Assent to their Acts of pretended Legislation:

For quartering large bodies of armed troops among us:

For protecting them, by a mock Trial, from Punishment for any Murders which they should commit on the Inhabitants of these States:

For cutting off our Trade with all parts of the world:

For imposing Taxes on us without our Consent:

For depriving us in many cases, of the benefits of Trial by Jury:

For transporting us beyond Seas to be tried for pretended offences:

For abolishing the free System of English Laws in a neighbouring Province, establishing therein an Arbitrary government, and enlarging its Boundaries so as to render it at once an example and fit instrument for introducing the same absolute rule into these Colonies:

For taking away our Charters, abolishing our most valuable Laws, and altering fundamentally the Forms of our Governments:

For suspending our own Legislatures, and declaring themselves invested with Power to legislate for us in all cases whatsoever.

He has abdicated Government here, by declaring us out of his Protection and waging War against us.

He has plundered our seas, ravaged our Coasts, burnt our towns, and destroyed the lives of our people.

He is at this time transporting large Armies of foreign Mercenaries to compleat the works of death, desolation and tyranny, already begun with circumstances of Cruelty & perfidy scarcely paralleled in the most barbarous ages, and totally unworthy the Head of a civilized nation.

He has constrained our fellow Citizens taken Captive on the high Seas to bear Arms against their Country, to become the executioners of their friends and Brethren, or to fall themselves by their Hands.

He has excited domestic insurrections amongst us, and has endeavoured to bring on the inhabitants of our frontiers, the merciless Indian Savages, whose known rule of warfare, is an undistinguished destruction of all ages, sexes and conditions.

In every stage of these Oppressions We have Petitioned for Redress in the most humble terms: Our repeated Petitions have been answered only by repeated injury. A Prince whose character is thus marked by every act which may define a Tyrant, is unfit to be the ruler of a free people.

Nor have We been wanting in attentions to our British brethren. We have warned them from time to time of attempts by their legislature to extend an unwarrantable jurisdiction over us. We have reminded them of the circumstances of our emigration and settlement here. We have appealed to their native justice and magnanimity, and we have conjured them by the ties of our common kindred to disavow these usurpations, which, would inevitably interrupt our connections and correspondence. They too have been deaf to the voice of justice and of consanguinity. We must, therefore, acquiesce in the necessity, which denounces our Separation, and hold them, as we hold the rest of mankind, Enemies in War, in Peace Friends.

We, therefore, the Representatives of the united States of America, in General Congress, Assembled, appealing to the Supreme Judge of the world for the rectitude of our intentions, do, in the Name, and by Authority of the good People of these Colonies, solemnly publish and declare, That these United Colonies are, and of Right ought to be Free and Independent States; that they are Absolved from all Allegiance to the British Crown, and that all political connection between them and the State of Great Britain, is and ought to be totally dissolved; and that as Free and Independent States, they have full Power to levy War, conclude Peace, contract Alliances, establish Commerce, and to do all other Acts and Things which Independent States may of right do. And for the support of this Declaration, with a firm reliance on the protection of divine Providence, we mutually pledge to each other our Lives, our Fortunes and our sacred Honor.

Source: Francis Newton Thorpe, ed., *The Federal and State Constitutions, Colonial Charters and Other Organic Laws* (Washington, 1909), 1 :3–6.

4.

Writing the American Constitution

Writing the Constitution was a lengthy process that began in the American Revolution. In some ways it extends to this day, as we continue to interpret and reinterpret the document written in 1787.

The first American constitutions came from the states and were written in the midst of war. These documents strengthened legislative assemblies at the expense of the governors. Pennsylvania even did away with the office of governor altogether. To really understand American constitutionalism during this period, it is to the states we must turn and not the national document. The Articles of Confederation recognized the primacy of the states. Critics of the Articles have sometimes ridiculed our first constitution as impossibly weak. In fact, given the revolutionaries' commitment to small-scale republicanism, no other document could have been produced in those historical circumstances. The Revolutionary War pitted the colonies/states against an imperial authority. Naturally, the revolutionaries believed real democracy was only possible at the state or even neighborhood level. They had good reason to distrust distant national authorities.

In the 1780s some Americans, it is not possible to know how many, became disenchanted with how the states used the sovereignty so carefully left in their hands by the Articles. James Madison and others complained that the states changed their laws too freely, creating an unstable situation where it was difficult to know what the law actually was from one term to the next. It is significant that Madison did not feel that the state legislatures protected the property of those with wealth. To the contrary, Madison and his friends feared that the states actually had proved overly protective of debtors' rights. This threatened the rights of creditors.

At Madison's urging, the states (with the exception of Rhode Island) sent delegates to a convention in Philadelphia supposedly to revise the Articles but really to write a new constitution. The assembled delegates considered the Virginia Plan, which proposed granting Congress sweeping, even breathtaking, new powers. Speaking through the Virginia Plan, Madison even urged giving Congress the power to veto acts of the state legislature. And he wanted the national government to have the power to use military force ("the force of the Union") against misbehaving states.

The New Jersey Plan sought to protect states' rights by giving Congress only enumerated powers, a list of things it could do. Whether there really was a states' rights faction at the Philadelphia convention is a matter of debate. The most ardent protectors of states' rights, Patrick Henry and Sam Adams, refused to attend. Henry famously declared he "smelled a rat." It may be that the authors of the New Jersey Plan simply doubted they could sell the provisions of the Virginia Plan to the voters back home. They may have offered the New Jersey Plan because they thought it more truly reflected what most voters would support. In any case, the delegates swiftly rejected the New Jersey Plan, though a look at Article I, Section 8, reveals they did not entirely repudiate enumerated powers.

The fight over ratifying the Constitution produced the *Federalist Papers*, the most brilliant exegesis of the framers' principles available. Written primarily by James Madison and Alexander Hamilton, the *Federalist Papers* explained the rationale for establishing such a powerful national government, one expressly made superior to the states.

Antifederalist opponents of the Constitution offered a variety of arguments against ratification. Their most powerful sword came in the form of a complaint that the document included no bill of rights. The state constitutions had bills of rights, they pointed out, why not the national constitution? The Federalists answered that the Constitution did not threaten individual rights, but the Antifederalists, while unable to prevent ratification, won the argument over a bill of rights. Ironically, they managed to compel the foremost Federalist, James Madison, to usher the Bill of Rights through Congress. In 1791, the necessary number of states ratified the Bill of Rights and it became part of the Constitution.

State Constitutions (1776)

Breaking ties with England meant, among other things, establishing frameworks for governing the newly launched United States of America. The former colonies, now states, wrote constitutions that served as the fundamental organic law in the new nation until the ratification of the national Constitution in 1789. These documents reflected Americans' concepts of how government should work in the still-experimental republic. The new state constitutions reveal a reaction against the powerful colonial governors who, under the old regime, had represented the interests of the crown rather than the colonies. Many states stripped the governor of crucial powers, allocating most authority to the state legislatures instead. In many plans, governors were elected by the legislature and allowed to serve terms of only one year. Most provided for the impeachment of the governor, a device nearly unheard of in England. Virginia's constitution provides an example of the process of constitution-building in the new republic.

Constitution of Virginia, 1776

WE, therefore, the delegates and representatives of the good people of Virginia...do ordain and declare the future form of government of Virginia to be as followeth:

The legislative, executive, and judiciary department, shall be separate and distinct, so that neither exercise the powers properly belonging to the other: nor shall any person exercise the powers of more than one of them, at the same time; except that the Justices of the County Courts shall be eligible to either House of Assembly.

The legislative shall be formed of two distinct branches, who, together, shall be a complete Legislature. They shall meet once, or oftener, every year, and shall be called, *The General Assembly of Virginia*. One of these shall be called, *The House of Delegates*, and consist of two Representatives, to be chosen for each county, and for the district of West-Augusta, annually, of such men as actually reside in, and are freeholders of the same, or duly qualified according to law, and also of one Delegate or Representative, to be chosen annually for the city of Williamsburgh, and one for the borough of Norfolk, and a Representative for each of such other cities and boroughs, as may hereafter be allowed particular representation by the legislature; but when any city or borough shall so decrease, as that the number of persons, having right of suffrage therein, shall have been, for the space of seven years successively, less than half the number of voters in some one county in Virginia, such city or borough thenceforward shall cease to send a Delegate or Representative to the Assembly.

The other shall be called *The Senate*, and consist of twenty-four members of whom thirteen shall constitute a House to proceed on business; for whose election, the different counties shall be divided into twenty-four districts; and each county of the respective district, at the time of the election of its Delegates, shall vote for one Senator, who is actually a resident and freeholder within the district, or duly qualified according to law, and is upwards of twenty-five years of age; and the Sheriffs of each county, within five days at farthest, after the last county election in the district, shall meet at some convenient place, and from the poll, so taken in their respective counties, return, as a Senator, the man who shall have the greatest number of votes in the whole district. To keep up this Assembly by rotation, the districts shall be equally divided into four classes and numbered by lot. At the end of one year after the general election, the six members, elected by the first division, shall be displaced, and the vacancies thereby occasioned supplied from such class or division, by new election, in the manner aforesaid. This rotation shall be applied to each division, according to its number, and continued in due order annually....

A Governor, or chief magistrate, shall be chosen annually by joint ballot of both Houses (to be taken in each House respectively) deposited in the conference room; the boxes examined jointly by a committee of each House, and the numbers severally reported to them, that the appointments may be entered (which shall be the mode of taking the joint ballot of both Houses, in all cases) who shall not continue in that office longer than three years successively, nor be eligible, until the expiration of four years after he shall have been out of that office. An adequate, but moderate salary shall be settled on him, during his continuance in office; and he shall, with the advice of a Council of State, exercise the executive powers of government, according to the laws of this Commonwealth; and shall not, under any pretence, exercise any power or prerogative, by virtue of any law, statute or custom of England. But he shall, with the advice of the Council of State, have the power of granting reprieves or pardons, except where the prosecution shall have been carried on by the House of Delegates, or the law shall otherwise particularly direct; in which cases, no reprieve or pardon shall be granted, but by resolve of the House of Delegates.

Either House of the General Assembly may adjourn themselves respectively. The Governor shall not prorogue or adjourn the Assembly, during their sitting, nor dissolve them at any time; but he shall, if necessary, either by advice of the Council of State, or on application of a majority of the House of Delegates, call them before the time to which they shall stand prorogued or adjourned.

A Privy Council, or Council of State, consisting of eight members, shall be chosen, by joint ballot of both Houses of Assembly, either from their own members or the people at large, to assist in the administration of government. They shall annually choose, out of their own members, a President, who, in case of death, inability, or absence of the Governor from the government, shall act as Lieutenant-Governor. Four members shall be sufficient to act, and their advice and proceedings shall be entered on record, and signed by the members present, (to any part whereof, any member may enter his dissent) to be laid before the General Assembly, when called for by them. This Council may appoint their own Clerk, who shall have a salary settled by law, and take an oath of secrecy, in such matters as he shall be directed by the board to conceal. A sum of money, appropriated to that purpose, shall be divided annually among the members, in proportion to their attendance; and they shall be incapable, during their continuance in office, of sitting in either House of Assembly. Two members shall be removed, by joint ballot of both Houses of Assembly, at the end of every three years, and be ineligible for the three next years. These vacancies, as well as those occasioned by death or incapacity, shall be supplied by new elections, in the same manner.

The Delegates for Virginia to the Continental Congress shall be chosen annually, or superseded in the mean time, by joint ballot of both Houses of Assembly....

The Governor may embody the militia, with the advice of the Privy Council; and when embodied, shall alone have the direction of the militia, under the laws of the country.

The two Houses of Assembly shall, by joint ballot, appoint Judges of the Supreme Court of Appeals, and General Court, Judges in Chancery, Judges of Admiralty, Secretary, and the Attorney-General, to be commissioned by the Governor, and continue in office during good behaviour. In case of death, incapacity, or resignation, the Governor, with the advice of the Privy Council, shall appoint persons to succeed in office, to be approved or displaced by both Houses. These officers shall have fixed and adequate salaries, and, together with all others, holding lucrative offices, and all ministers of the gospel, of every denomination, be incapable of being elected members of either House of Assembly or the Privy Council....

A Treasurer shall be appointed annually, by joint ballot of both Houses....

Source: Francis Newton Thorpe, ed., *The Federal and State Constitutions, Colonial Charters, and Other Organic Laws* (Washington, 1909), 7:3815–3818.

The Articles of Confederation (1777)

States established frameworks for governing the new nation, but meanwhile a war for independence had to be waged. The Second Continental Congress served as the legislative body for the new republic as a whole but lacked the legal au-

thority to do so. The Articles of Confederation therefore provided Congress with enough powers to wage war, conduct diplomacy, and fulfill otherwise "external" duties – but little else. The bulk of internal governance was left to the states.

Nov. 15, 1777

Articles of Confederation and perpetual Union between the states of New Hampshire, Massachusetts-bay, Rhode Island and Providence Plantations, Connecticut, New-York, New-Jersey, Pennsylvania, Delaware, Maryland, Virginia, North-Carolina, South-Carolina and Georgia.

ARTICLE I. The Stile of this Confederacy shall be "The United States of America."

ARTICLE II. Each State retains its sovereignty, freedom, and independence, and every power, jurisdiction, and right, which is not by this confederation expressly delegated to the United States, in Congress assembled.

ARTICLE III. The said States hereby severally enter into a firm league of friendship with each other, for their common defense, the security of their liberties, and their mutual and general welfare, binding themselves to assist each other, against all force offered to, or attacks made upon them, or any of them, on account of religion, sovereignty, trade, or any other pretence whatever.

ARTICLE IV. The better to secure and perpetuate mutual friendship and intercourse among the people of the different States in this Union, the free inhabitants of each of these States, paupers, vagabonds, and fugitives from justice excepted, shall be entitled to all privileges and immunities of free citizens in the several States; and the people of each State shall have free ingress and regress to and from any other State, and shall enjoy therein all the privileges of trade and commerce, subject to the same duties, impositions, and restrictions as the inhabitants thereof respectively, provided that such restrictions shall not extend so far as to prevent the removal of property imported into any State, to any other State, of which the owner is an inhabitant; provided also that no imposition, duties or restriction shall be laid by any State, on the property of the United States, or either of them.

If any person guilty of, or charged with, treason, felony, or other high misdemeanor in any State, shall flee from justice, and be found in any of the United States, he shall upon demand of the Governor or Executive power of the State from which he fled, be delivered up and removed to the State having jurisdiction of his offence.

Full faith and credit shall be given in each of these States to the records, acts, and judicial proceedings of the courts and magistrates of every other State.

ARTICLE V. For the most convenient management of the general interests of the United States, delegates shall be annually appointed in such manner as the legislatures of each State shall direct, to meet in Congress on the first Monday in November, in every year, with a power reserved to each State to recall its delegates, or any of them, at any time within the year, and to send others in their stead for the remainder of the year.

No State shall be represented in Congress by less than two, nor more than seven members; and no person shall be capable of being a delegate for more than three years in any term of six years; nor shall any person, being a delegate, be capable of holding any office under the United States, for which he, or another for his benefit, receives any salary, fees or emolument of any kind.

Each State shall maintain its own delegates in a meeting of the States, and while they act as members of the committee of the States.

In determining questions in the United States in Congress assembled, each State shall have one vote.

Freedom of speech and debate in Congress shall not be impeached or questioned in any court, or place out of Congress, and the members of Congress shall be protected in their persons from arrests or imprisonments, during the time of their going to and from, and attendance on Congress, except for treason, felony, or breach of the peace.

ARTICLE VI. No State without the consent of the United States in Congress assembled, shall send any embassy to, or receive any embassy from, or enter into any conference, agreement, alliance or treaty with any king, prince or state; nor shall any person holding any office of profit or trust under the United States, or any of them, accept of any present, emolument, office or title of any kind whatever from any King, Prince or foreign State; nor shall the United States in Congress assembled, or any of them, grant any title of nobility.

No two or more States shall enter into any treaty, confederation or alliance whatever between them, without the consent of the United States in Congress assembled, specifying accurately the purposes for which the same is to be entered into, and how long it shall continue.

No State shall lay any imposts or duties, which may interfere with any stipulations in treaties, entered into by the United States in Congress assembled, with any King, Prince or State, in pursuance of any treaties already proposed by Congress, to the courts of France and Spain.

No vessel of war shall be kept up in time of peace by any State, except such number only, as shall be deemed necessary by the United States in Congress assembled, for the defense of such State, or its trade; nor shall any body of forces be kept up by any State in time of peace, except such number only, as in the judgment of the United States, in Congress assembled, shall be deemed requisite to garrison the forts necessary for the defence of such State; but every State shall always keep up a well regulated and disciplined militia, sufficiently armed and accoutred, and shall provide and constantly have ready for use, in public stores, a due number of field pieces and tents, and a proper quantity of arms, ammunition and camp equipage.

No State shall engage in any war without the consent of the United States in Congress assembled, unless such State be actually invaded by enemies, or shall have received certain advice of a resolution being formed by some nation of Indians to invade such State, and the danger is so imminent as not to admit of a delay till the United States in Congress assembled can be consulted: nor shall any State grant commissions to any ships or vessels of war, nor letters of marque or reprisal, except it be after a declaration of war by the United States in Congress assembled, and then only against the kingdom or state and the subjects thereof, against which war has been so declared, and under such regulations as shall be established by the United States in Congress assembled, unless such State be infested by pirates, in which case vessels of war may be fitted out for that occasion, and kept so long as the danger shall continue, or until the United States in Congress assembled shall determine otherwise.

ARTICLE VII. When land-forces are raised by any State for the common defence, all officers of or under the rank of colonel, shall be appointed by the Legislature of each State respectively, by whom such forces shall be raised, or in such manner as such State shall direct, and all vacancies shall be filled up by the State which first made the appointment.

ARTICLE VIII. All charges of war, and all other expenses that shall be incurred for the common defence or general welfare, and allowed by the United States in Congress assembled, shall be defrayed out of a common treasury, which shall be supplied by the several States, in proportion to the value of all land within each State, granted or surveyed for any person, as such land and the buildings and improvements thereon shall be estimated according to such mode as the United States in Congress assembled, shall from time to time direct and appoint.

The taxes for paying that proportion shall be laid and levied by the authority and direction of the Legislatures of the several States within the time agreed upon by the United States in Congress assembled.

ARTICLE IX. The United States in Congress assembled, shall have the sole and exclusive right and power of determining on peace and war, except in the cases mentioned in the sixth article—of sending and receiving ambassadors—entering into treaties and alliances, provided that no treaty of commerce shall be made whereby the legislative power of the respective States shall be restrained from imposing such imposts and duties on foreigners, as their own people are subjected to, or from prohibiting the exportation or importation of any species of goods or commodities whatsoever—of establishing rules for deciding in all cases, what captures on land or water shall be legal, and in what manner prizes taken by land or naval forces in the service of the United States shall be divided or appropriated—of granting letters of marque and reprisal in times of peace—appointing courts for the trial of piracies and felonies committed on the high seas and establishing courts for receiving and determining finally appeals in all cases of captures, provided that no member of Congress shall be appointed a judge of any of the said courts.

The United States in Congress assembled shall also be the last resort on appeal in all disputes and differences now subsisting or that hereafter may arise between two or more States concerning boundary, jurisdiction or any other causes whatever; which authority shall always be exercised in the manner following. Whenever the legislative or executive authority or lawful agent of any State in controversy with another shall present a petition to Congress, stating the matter in question and praying for a hearing, notice thereof shall be given by order of Congress to the legislative or executive authority of the other State in controversy, and a day assigned for the appearance of the parties by their lawful agents, who shall then be directed to appoint by joint consent, commissioners or judges to constitute a court for hearing and determining the matter in question: but if they cannot agree, Congress shall name three persons out of each of the United States, and from the list of such persons each party shall alternately strike out one, the petitioners beginning, until the number shall be reduced to thirteen; and from that number not less than seven, nor more than nine names as Congress shall direct, shall in the presence of Congress be drawn out by lot, and the persons whose names shall be so drawn or any five of them, shall be commissioners or judges, to hear and finally determine the controversy, so always as a major part of the judges who shall hear the cause shall agree in the determination: and if either party shall neglect to attend at the day appointed, without showing reasons, which Congress shall judge sufficient, or being present shall refuse to strike, the Congress shall proceed to nominate three persons out of each State, and the secretary of Congress shall strike in behalf of such party absent or refusing; and the judgment and sentence of the court to be appointed, in the manner before prescribed, shall be final and conclusive; and if any of the parties shall refuse to submit to the authority of such court, or to appear or defend their claim or cause, the court shall nevertheless proceed to pronounce sentence, or judgment, which shall in like manner be final and decisive, the judgment or sentence and other proceedings being in either case transmitted to Congress, and lodged among the acts of Congress for the security of the parties concerned: provided that every commissioner, before he sits in judgment, shall take an oath to be administered by one of the judges of the supreme or superior court of the State where the cause shall be tried, "well and truly to hear and determine the matter in question, according to the best of his judgment, without favor, affection or hope of reward:" provided also, that no State shall be deprived of territory for the benefit of the United States.

All controversies concerning the private right of soil claimed under different grants of two or more States, whose jurisdictions as they may respect such lands, and the States which passed such grants are adjusted, the said grants or either of them being at the same time claimed to have originated antecedent to such settlement of jurisdiction, shall on the petition of either party to the Congress of the United States, be finally determined as near as may be in the same manner as is before prescribed for deciding disputes respecting territorial jurisdiction between different States.

The United States in Congress assembled shall also have the sole and exclusive right and power of regulating the alloy and value of coin struck by their own authority, or by that of the re-spective States. — fixing the standards of weights and measures throughout the United States. — regulating the trade and manag-ing all affairs with the Indians, not members of any of the States, provided that the legislative right of any State within its own lim-its be not infringed or violated — establishing and regulating post-offices from one State to another, throughout all the United States, and exacting such postage on the papers passing through the same as may be requisite to defray the expenses of the said of-fice — appointing all officers of the land forces, in the service of the United States, excepting regimental officers — appointing all the officers of the naval forces, and commissioning all officers what-ever in the service of the United States — making rules for the gov-ernment and regulation of the said land and naval forces, and di-recting their operations.

The United States in Congress assembled shall have authority to appoint a committee, to sit in the recess of Congress, to be de-nominated "A Committee of the States," and to consist of one delegate from each State; and to appoint such other committees and civil officers as may be necessary for managing the general af-fairs of the United States under their direction — to appoint one of their members to preside, provided that no person be allowed to serve in the office of president more than one year in any term of three years; to ascertain the necessary sums of money to be raised for the service of the United States, and to appropriate and apply the same for defraying the public expenses — to borrow money, or emit bills on the credit of the United States, transmitting every half-year to the respective States an account of the sums of money so borrowed or emitted, — to build and equip a navy — to agree upon the number of land forces, and to make requisitions from each State for its quota, in proportion to the number of white in-habitants in such State; which requisition shall be binding, and thereupon the legislature of each State shall appoint the regimen-tal officers, raise the men and cloath, arm and equip them in a sol-dier-like manner, at the expense of the United States; and the offi-cers and men so cloathed, armed and equipped shall march to the place appointed, and within the time agreed on by the United

States in Congress assembled: but if the United States in Congress assembled shall, on consideration of circumstances judge proper that any State should not raise men, or should raise a smaller number of men than the quota thereof, such extra number shall be raised, officered, cloathed, armed and equipped in the same manner as the quota of each State, unless the legislature of such State shall judge that such extra number cannot be safely spread out in the same, in which case they shall raise, officer, cloath, arm and equip as many of such extra number as they judge can be safely spared. And the officers and men so cloathed, armed, and equipped, shall march to the place appointed, and within the time agreed on by the United States in Congress assembled.

The United States in Congress assembled shall never engage in a war, nor grant letters of marque or reprisal in time of peace, nor enter into any treaties or alliances, nor coin money, nor regulate the value thereof, nor ascertain the sums and expenses necessary for the defense and welfare of the United States, or any of them, nor emit bills, nor borrow money on the credit of the United States, nor appropriate money, nor agree upon the number of vessels of war, to be built or purchased, or the number of land or sea forces to be raised, nor appoint a commander in chief of the army or navy, unless nine States assent to the same: nor shall a question on any other point, except for adjourning from day to day be determined, unless by the votes of the majority of the United States in Congress assembled.

The Congress of the United States shall have power to adjourn to any time within the year, and to any place within the United States, so that no period of adjournment be for a longer duration than the space of six months, and shall publish the journal of their proceedings monthly, except such parts thereof relating to treaties, alliances or military operations, as in their judgment require secrecy; and the yeas and nays of the delegates of each State on any question shall be entered on the journal, when it is desired by any delegates of a State, or any of them, at his or their request shall be furnished with a transcript of the said journal, except such parts as are above excepted, to lay before the Legislatures of the several States.

ARTICLE X. The committee of the States, or any nine of them, shall be authorized to execute, in the recess of Congress, such of the powers of Congress as the United States in Congress assembled, by the consent of the nine States, shall from time to time think expedient to vest them with; provided that no power be delegated to the said committee, for the exercise of which, by the articles of confederation, the voice of nine States in the Congress of the United States assembled be requisite.

ARTICLE XI. Canada acceding to this confederation, and adjoining in the measures of the United States, shall be admitted into, and entitled to all the advantages of this Union: but no other colony shall be admitted into the same, unless such admission be agreed to by nine States.

ARTICLE XII. All bills of credit emitted, monies borrowed and debts contracted by, or under the authority of Congress, before the assembling of the United States, in pursuance of the present confederation, shall be deemed and considered as a charge against the United States, for payment and satisfaction whereof the said United States, and the public faith are hereby solemnly pledged.

ARTICLE XIII. Every State shall abide by the determination of the United States in Congress assembled, on all questions which by this confederation are submitted to them. And the articles of this confederation shall be inviolably observed by every State, and the Union shall be perpetual; nor shall any alteration at any time hereafter be made in any of them; unless such alteration be agreed to in a Congress of the United States, and be afterwards confirmed by the Legislatures of every State.

And whereas it hath pleased the Great Governor of the World to incline the hearts of the Legislatures we respectively represent in Congress, to approve of, and to authorize us to ratify the said articles of confederation and perpetual union. Know Ye that we the undersigned delegates, by virtue of the power and authority to us given for that purpose, do by these presents, in the name and in behalf of our respective constituents, fully and entirely ratify and confirm each and every of the said articles of confederation and perpetual union, and all and singular the matters and things therein contained: And we do further solemnly plight and engage the faith of our respective constituents, that they shall abide by the determinations of the United States in Congress assembled, on all questions, which by the said Confederation are submitted to them. And that the Articles thereof shall be inviolably observed by the States we respectively represent, and that the Union shall be perpetual.

In Witness whereof we have hereunto set our hands in Congress. Done at Philadelphia in the State of Pennsylvania the ninth day of July in the Year of our Lord One Thousand Seven Hundred and Seventy-Eight, and in the Third Year of the independence of America.

In force after ratification by Maryland, 1 March 1781

Source: Francis Newton Thorpe, ed., *The Federal and State Constitutions, Colonial Charters, and Other Organic Laws* (Washington, 1909), 1:9–16.

Vices of the Political System of the U. States (1787)
James Madison

After a long and bloody struggle to break away from England, the heady expectations of revolution began to give way to disappointment, fear, and doubt for many Americans. The young nation was beset by severe economic problems and the states–used to centuries of acting autonomously in their own interests--squabbled among themselves. Weak by design, the national government could do very little to right the country's course. Virginian James Madison articulated the frustrations Americans experienced in the early years of independence.

Observations by J. M.

1. *Failure of the States to comply with the Constitutional requisitions:* This evil has been so fully experienced both during the war and since the peace, results so naturally from the number and

independent authority of the States and has been so uniformly exemplified in every similar Confederacy, that it may be considered as not less radically and permanently inherent in than it is fatal to the object of, the present system.

2. *Encroachments by the States on the federal authority:* Examples of this are numerous and repetitions may be foreseen in almost every case where any favorite object of a State shall present a temptation. Among these examples are the wars and Treaties of Georgia with the Indians, the unlicensed compacts between Virginia and Maryland, and between Pena. & N. Jersey the troops raised and to be kept up by Massts....

4. *Trespasses of the States on the rights of each other:* These are alarming symptoms, and may be daily apprehended as we are admonished by daily experience. See the law of Virginia restricting foreign vessels to certain ports; of Maryland in favor of vessels belonging to her *own citizens*; of N. York in favor of the same.

Paper money, installments of debts, occlusion of courts, making property a legal tender, may likewise be deemed aggressions on the rights of other States. As the Citizens of every State, aggregately taken, stand more or less in the relation of creditors or debtors to the Citizens of every other State, acts of the debtor State in favor of debtors affect the creditor State in the same manner as they do its own citizens, who are, relatively, creditors towards other citizens. This remark may be extended to foreign nations. If the exclusive regulation of the value and alloy of coin was properly delegated to the federal authority, the policy of it equally requires a controul on the States in the cases above mentioned. It must have been meant—1. To preserve uniformity in the circulating medium throughout the nation 2. To prevent those frauds on the citizens of other States, and the subjects of foreign powers, which might disturb the tranquility at home, or involve the Union in foreign contests.

The practice of many States in restricting the commercial intercourse with other States, and putting their productions and manufactures on the same footing with those of foreign nations, though not contrary to the federal articles, is certainly adverse to the spirit of the Union, and tends to beget retaliating regulations, not less expensive & vexatious in themselves, than they are destructive of the general harmony....

8. *Want of ratification by the people of the articles of Confederation*: In some of the States the Confederation is recognized by and forms a part of the constitution. In others, however, it has received no other sanction than that of the legislative authority. From this defect two evils result: 1. Whenever a law of a State happens to be repugnant to an act of Congress, particularly when the latter is of posterior date to the former, it will be at least questionable whether the latter must not prevail; and as the question must be decided by the Tribunals of the State, they will be most likely to lean on the side of the State.

    As far as the union of the States is to be regarded as a league of sovereign powers, and not as a political Constitution, by virtue of which they are become one sovereign power, so far it seems to follow, from the doctrine of compacts, that a breach of any of the articles of the Confederation by any of the parties to it absolves the other parties from their respective obligations, and gives them a right if they choose to exert it, of dissolving the Union altogether.

9. *Multiplicity of laws in the several States:* ...Among the evils, then, of our situation, may well be ranked the multiplicity of laws from which no State is exempt. As far as laws are necessary to mark with precision the duties of those who are to obey them, and to take from those who are to administer them a discretion which might be abused, their number is the price of liberty. As far as the laws exceed this limit they are a nuisance; a nuisance of the most pestilent kind....

10. *Mutability of the laws of the States:* This evil is intimately connected with the former, yet deserves a distinct notice as it emphatically denotes a vicious legislation. We daily see laws repealed or superseded before any trial can have been made of their merits; and even before a knowledge of them can have reached the remoter districts within which they were to operate....

11. *Injustice of the laws of States:* If the multiplicity and mutability of laws prove a want of wisdom, their injustice betrays a defect still more alarming; more alarming, not merely because it is a greater evil in itself, but because it brings more into question the fundamental principle of republican Government, that the majority who rule in such Governments, are the safest Guardians both of public Good and of private rights. To what causes is this evil to be ascribed?

These causes lie — 1. In the representative bodies. 2. In the people themselves.

1. Representative appointments are sought from 3 motives. 1. Ambition 2. Personal interest. 3. Public good. Unhappily, the two first are proved by experience to be most prevalent. Hence, the candidates who feel them, particularly, the second, are most industrious, and most successful in pursuing their object; and forming often a majority in the legislative Councils, with interested views, contrary to the interest, and views, of their constituents, join in a perfidious sacrifice of the latter to the former....

2. A still more fatal, if not more frequent cause, lies among the people themselves. All civilized societies are divided into different interests and factions, as they happen to be creditors or debtors, rich or poor, husbandmen, merchants or manufacturers, members of different religious sects, followers of different political leaders, inhabitants of different districts, owners of different kinds of property, &c., &c. In republican Government, the majority, however composed, ultimately give the law. Whenever therefore an apparent interest or common passion unites a majority, what is to restrain them from unjust violations of the rights and interests of the minority, or of individuals?...If an enlargement of the sphere is found to lessen the insecurity of private rights, it is not because the impulse of a common interest or passion is less predominant in this case with the majority, but because a common interest or passion is less apt to be felt, and the requisite combinations less easy to be formed, by a great than by a small number. The society becomes broken into a greater variety of interests of pursuits of

passions, which check each other, whilst those who may feel a common sentiment have less opportunity of communication and concert. It may be inferred that the inconveniences of popular States contrary to the prevailing Theory, are in proportion not to the extent, but to the narrowness of their limits....

Source: Letters and Other Writings of James Madison, Fourth President of the United States, 4 vols. (New York, 1884), 1:320–321, 322–323. 324–327.

The Constitutional Convention (1787)

Although they were taking the extraordinary step of reconstituting the national government, delegates to the constitutional convention met in secret, and no official stenographer transcribed the proceedings. Today, our best source for understanding what transpired during those difficult sixteen weeks in Philadelphia is James Madison's personal notes. In them we get a fascinating glimpse into the founders' thinking about the nature and practice of governing. Among other revelations, the notes describe differing models for the structure and functions of the national government and enable us to detect the series of compromises that became what we now think of as "the" United States Constitution. While the "Virginia Plan" proposed by Edmund Randolph (but mostly written by James Madison) designed a national authority with broad, general authorities, Madison even wanted the national congress to have the power to veto acts of the state legislatures. The "New Jersey Plan" would have protected the states by limiting the powers to certain enumerated powers.

Virginia Plan

May 29, 1787

1. Resolved that the Articles of Confederation ought to be so corrected & enlarged as to accomplish the objects proposed by their institution; namely, "common defence, security of liberty and general welfare."

2. Resd. therefore that the rights of suffrage in the National Legislature ought to be proportioned to the Quotas of contribution, or to the number of free inhabitants, as the one or the other rule may seem best in different cases.
3. Resd. that the National Legislature ought to consist of two branches.
4. Resd. that the members of the first branch of the National Legislature ought to be elected by the people of the several States every _____ for the term of _____; to be of the age of _____ years at least, to receive liberal stipends by which they may be compensated for the devotion of their time to public service; to be ineligible to any office established by a particular State, or under the authority of the United States, except those peculiarly belonging to the functions of the first branch, during the term of service, and for the space of _____ after its expiration; to be incapable of re-election for the space of _____ after the expiration of their term of service, and to be subject to recall.
5. Resold. that the members of the second branch of the National Legislature ought to be elected by those of the first, out of a proper number of persons nominated by the individual Legislatures, to be of the age of _____ years at least; to hold their offices for a term sufficient to ensure their independency; to receive liberal stipends, by which they may be compensated for the devotion of their time to public service; and to be ineligible to any office established by a particular State, or under the authority of the United States, except those peculiarly belonging to the functions of the second branch, during the term of service, and for the space of _____ after the expiration thereof.
6. Resolved that each branch ought to possess the right of originating Acts; that the National Legislature ought to be impowered to enjoy the Legislative Rights vested in Congress by the Confederation & moreover to legislate in all cases to which the separate States are incompetent, or in which the harmony of the United States may be interrupted by the exercise of individual Legislation; to negative all laws passed by the several States, contravening in the opinion of the National Legislature the articles of Union; and to call forth the force of the Union

agst. any member of the Union failing to fulfill its duty under the articles thereof.

7. Resd. that a National Executive be instituted; to be chosen by the National Legislature for the term of _____ years, to receive punctually at stated times, a fixed compensation for the services rendered, in which no increase or diminution shall be made so as to affect the Magistracy, existing at the time of increase or diminution, and to be ineligible a second time; and that besides a general authority to execute the National laws, it ought to enjoy the Executive rights vested in Congress by the Confederation.

8. Resd. that the Executive and a convenient number of the National Judiciary, ought to compose a council of revision with authority to examine every act of the National Legislature before it shall operate, & every act of a particular Legislature before a Negative thereon shall be final; and that the dissent of the said Council shall amount to a rejection, unless the Act of the National Legislature be again passed, or that of a particular Legislature be again negatived by _____ of the members of each branch.

9. Resd. that a National Judiciary be established to consist of one or more supreme tribunals, and of inferior tribunals to be chosen by the National Legislature, to hold their offices during good behaviour; and to receive punctually at stated times fixed compensation for their services, in which no increase or diminution shall be made so as to affect the persons actually in office at the time of such increase or diminution. That the jurisdiction of the inferior tribunals shall be to hear & determine in the first instance, and of the supreme tribunal to hear and determine in the dernier resort, all piracies & felonies on the high seas, captures from an enemy; cases in which foreigners or citizens of other States applying to such jurisdictions may be interested, or which respect the collection of the National revenue; impeachments of any National officers, and questions which may involve the national peace and harmony.

10. Resolvd. that provision ought to be made for the admission of States lawfully arising within the limits of the United States,

whether from a voluntary junction of Government & Territory or otherwise, with the consent of a number of voices in the National legislature less than the whole.

11. Resd. that a Republican Government & the territory of each State, except in the instance of a voluntary junction of Government & territory, ought to be guaranteed by the United States to each State.

12. Resd. that provision ought to be made for the continuance of Congress and their authorities and privileges, until a given day after the reform of the articles of Union shall be adopted, and for the completion of all their engagements.

13. Resd. that provision ought to be made for the amendment of the Articles of Union whensoever it shall seem necessary, and that the assent of the National Legislature ought not to be required thereto.

14. Resd. that the Legislative Executive & Judiciary powers within the several States ought to be bound by oath to support the articles of Union.

15. Resd. that the amendments which shall be offered to the Confederation, by the Convention ought at a proper time, or times, after the approbation of Congress to be submitted to an assembly or assemblies of Representatives, recommended by the several Legislatures to be expressly chosen by the people, to consider & decide thereon.

Source: Gaillard Hunt and James Brown Scott, eds. *Debates in the Federal Convention of 1787 Which Framed the Constitution of the United States of America, Reported by James Madison* (New York, 1920), 23–26.

New Jersey Plan

June 15th, 1787

The propositions from N. Jersey moved by Mr. Patterson were in the words following.

1. Resd. that the articles of Confederation ought to be so revised, corrected & enlarged, as to render the federal Constitution adequate to the exigences of Government, & the preservation of the Union.

2. Resd. that in addition to the powers vested in the U. States in Congress, by the present existing articles of Confederation, they be authorized to pass acts for raising a revenue, by levying a duty or duties on all goods or merchandizes of foreign growth or manufacture, imported into any part of the U. States, by Stamps on paper, vellum or parchment, and by a postage on all letters or packages passing through the general post-office, to be applied to such federal purposes as they shall deem proper & expedient; to make rules & regulations for the collection thereof; and the same from time to time, to alter & amend in such manner as they shall think proper: to pass Acts for the regulation of trade & commerce as well with foreign nations as with each other: provided that all punishments, fines, forfeitures & penalties to be incurred for contravening such acts rules and regulations shall be adjudged by the Common law Judiciarys of the State in which any offence contrary to the true intent & meaning of such Acts rules & regulations shall have been committed or perpetrated, with liberty of commencing in the first instance all suits & prosecutions for that purpose in the superior Common law Judiciary in such State, subject nevertheless, for the correction of all errors, both in law & fact in rendering Judgment, to an appeal to the Judiciary of the U. States.

3. Resd. that whenever requisitions shall be necessary, instead of the rule for making requisitions mentioned in the articles of Confederation, the United States in Congs. be authorized to make such requisitions in proportion to the whole number of white & other free citizens & inhabitants of every age sex and condition including those bound to servitude for a term of years & three fifths of all other persons not comprehended in the foregoing description, except Indians not paying taxes; that if such requisitions be not complied with, in the time specified therein, to direct the collection thereof in the non

complying States & for that purpose to devise and pass acts directing & authorizing the same; provided that none of the powers hereby vested in the U. States in Congs. shall be exercised without the consent of at least _____ States, and in that proportion if the number of Confederated States should hereafter be increased or diminished.

4. Resd. that the U. States in Congs. be authorized to elect a federal Executive to consist of _____ persons, to continue in office for the term of _____ years, to receive punctually at stated times a fixed compensation for their services, in which no increase or diminution shall be made so as to affect the persons composing the Executive at the time of such increase or diminution, to be paid out of the federal treasury; to be incapable of holding any other office or appointment during their time of service and for _____ years thereafter; to be ineligible a second time, & removeable by Congs. on application by a majority of the Executives of the several States; that the Executives besides their general authority to execute the federal acts ought to appoint all federal officers not otherwise provided for, & to direct all military operations; provided that none of the persons composing the federal Executive shall on any occasion take command of any troops, so as personally to conduct any enterprise as General, or in other capacity.

5. Resd. that a federal Judiciary be established to consist of a supreme Tribunal the Judges of which to be appointed by the Executive, & to hold their offices during good behaviour, to receive punctually at stated times a fixed compensation for their services in which no increase or diminution shall be made, so as to affect the persons actually in office at the time of such increase or diminution; that the Judiciary so established shall have authority to hear & determine in the first instance on all impeachments of federal officers, & by way of appeal in the dernier resort in all cases touching the rights of Ambassadors, in all cases of captures from an enemy, in all cases of piracies & felonies on the high Seas, in all cases in which foreigners may be interested, in the construction of any treaty or treaties, or which may arise on any of the Acts for

regulation of trade, or the collection of the federal Revenue: that none of the Judiciary shall during the time they remain in office be capable of receiving or holding any other office or appointment during their time of service, or for ____thereafter.

6. Resd. that all Acts of the U. States in Congs. made by virtue & in pursuance of the powers hereby & by the articles of Confederation vested in them, and all Treaties made & ratified under the authority of the U. States shall be the supreme law of the respective States so far forth as those Acts or Treaties shall relate to the said States or their Citizens, and that the Judiciary of the several States shall be bound thereby in their decisions, any thing in the respective laws of the Individual States to the contrary notwithstanding; and that if any State, or any body of men in any State shall oppose or prevent ye. carrying into execution such acts or treaties, the federal Executive shall be authorized to call forth ye. power of the Confederated States, or so much thereof as may be necessary to enforce and compel an obedience to such Acts, or an observance of such Treaties.

7. Resd. that provision be made for the admission of new States into the Union.

8. Resd. the rule for naturalization ought to be the same in every State.

9. Resd. that a Citizen of one State committing an offence in another State of the Union, shall be deemed guilty of the same offence as if it had been committed by a Citizen of the State in which the offence was committed.

Source: Gaillard Hunt and James Brown Scott, eds. *Debates in the Federal Convention of 1787 Which Framed the Constitution of the United States of America, Reported by James Madison* (New York, 1920), 102–104.

Both the Virginia and the New Jersey plans proposed creating the presidency. The delegates debated at some length how the new president would be chosen. Nationalists wanted the president elected directly by the people — so that president could claim more power as the people's representative. Delegates deter-

mined to protect the states' powers saw the danger in this and wanted the states to pick the president.

MR. WILSON made the following motion, to be substituted for the mode proposed by Mr. Randolph's resolution, "that the Executive Magistracy shall be elected in the following manner:

That the States be divided into__districts: & that the persons qualified to vote in each district for members of the first branch of the national Legislature elect__members for their respective districts to be electors of the Executive magistracy, that the said Electors of the Executive magistracy meet at____and they or any of them so met shall proceed to elect by ballot, but not our of their own body__person in whom the Executive authority of the national Government shall be vested."

MR. WILSON repeated his arguments in favor of an election without the intervention of the States. He supposed too that this mode would produce more confidence among the people in the first magistrate, than an election by the national Legislature.

MR. GERRY, opposed the election by the national legislature. There would be a constant intrigue, kept up for the appointment. The Legislature & the candidates wd. Bargain & play into one another's hands, votes would be given by the former under promises or expectations from the latter, of recompensing them by services to members of the Legislature or to their friends. He liked the principle of Mr. Wilson's motion, but fears it would alarm & give a handle to the State partisans, as tending to supersede altogether the State authorities. He thought the Community not yet ripe for stripping the States of their powers, even such as might not be requisite for local purposes. He was for waiting till people should feel more the necessity of it. He seemed to prefer the taking the suffrages of the States instead of Electors, or letting the Legislatures nominate, and the electors appoint. He was not clear that the people ought to act directly even in the choice of electors, being too little informed of personal characters in large districts, and liable to deceptions.

MR. WILLIAMSON could see no advantage in the introduction of Electors chosen by the people who would stand in the same relation to them as the State Legislatures, whilst the expedient would be attended with great trouble and expence.

On the question for agreeing to Mr. Wilson's substitute, it was negatived: Massts. no. Cont. no. N. Y. no. Pa. ay. Del. no. Mard. ay. Virga. no. N.C. no. S.C. no. Geoa. no.

On the question for electing the Executive by the national legislature, for the term of seven years, it was agreed to Massts. ay. Cont. ay. N. Y. ay. Pena. no. Del. ay. Maryd. no. Va. ay. N.C. ay. S. C. ay. Geo. ay....

SATURDAY JUNE 9th

MR. GERRY, according to previous notice given by him, moved "that the National Executive should be elected by the Executives of the States whose proportion of votes should be the same with that allowed to the States in the election of the senate." If the appointmt. Should be made by the Natl. Legislature, it would lessen that independence of the Executive which ought to prevail, would give birth to intrigue and corruption between the Executive & Legislature previous to the election, and to partiality in the Executive afterwards to the friends who promoted him. Some other mode therefore appeared to him necessary. He proposed that of appointing by the State Executives as most analogous to the principle observed in electing the other branches of the Natl. Govt.; the first branch being chosen by the *people* of the States, & the 2d. by the Legislatures of the States; he did not see any objection agst. letting the Executive be appointed by the Executives of the States. He supposed the Executives would be most likely to select the fittest men, and that it would be their interest to support the man of their own choice.

MR. RANDOLPH, urged strongly the inexpediency of Mr. Gerry's mode of appointing the Natl. Executive. The confidence of the people would not be secured by it to the Natl. magistrate. The small States would lose all chance of an appointmt. from within themselves. Bad appointments would be made; the Executives of the States being little conversant with characters not within their own small spheres. The State Executives too notwithstanding their constitutional independence, being in fact dependent on the State Legislatures will generally be guided by the views of the latter, and prefer either favorites within the States, or such as it may be expected will be most partial to the interests of the State. A Natl. Executive thus chosen will not be likely to defend with becoming vigilance & firmness the national rights agst. State encroachments. Vacancies also must happen. How can these be filled? He could not suppose either that the Executives would feel the interest in supporting the Natl. Executive which had been imagined. They will not cherish the great Oak which is to reduce them to paltry shrubs.

On the question for referring the appointment of the Natl. Executive to the State Executives as propd. By Mr. Gerry. Massts. no. Cont. no. N. Y. no. N.J. no. Geo. no. Pa. no. Del. divd. Md. no. Va. no. S. C. no.

MR. PATTERSON moves that the Committee resume the clause relating to the rule of suffrage in the Natl. Legislature.

MR. BREARLY seconds him. He was sorry he said that any question on this point was brought into view. It had been much agitated in Congs. at the time of forming the Confederation and was then rightly settled by allowing to each sovereign State an equal vote. Otherwise the smaller States must have been destroyed instead of being saved. ...

MR. PATTERSON considered the proposition for a proportional representation as striking at the existence of the lesser States. He wd. premise however to an investigation of this question some remarks on the nature structure and powers of the Convention...We ought to keep within its limits, or we should be charged by our Constituents with usurpation, that the people of America were sharpsighted and not to be deceived....We have no power to go beyond the federal scheme, and if we had the people are not ripe for any other. We must follow the people; the people will not follow us — The *proposition* could not be maintained whether considered in reference to us as a nation, or as a confederacy. A confederacy supposes sovereignty in the members composing it & sovereignty supposes equality. If we are to be considered as a nation, all State distinctions must be abolished, the whole must be thrown into hotchpot, and when an equal division is made, then there may be fairly and equality of representation. He held up Virga. Massts. & Pa. as the three large States, and the other ten as small ones; repeating the calculations of Mr. BREARLY as to the disparity of votes which wd. take place, and affirming that the small States would never agree to it. He said there was no more reason that a great individual State contributing much, should have more votes than a small one contributing little, than that a rich individual citizen should have more votes than an indigent one....

Source: Gaillard Hunt and James Brown Scott, eds., *The Debates in the Federal Convention of 1787 Which Framed the Constitution of the United States of America, Reported by James Madison* (New York, 1920), 41–43, 79–82.

The United States Constitution (1787)

In July 1787, after several grueling weeks of discussion and debate in the stifling heat of a Philadelphia summer, the delegates selected a committee of detail to draft a new national constitution. Further debate ensued, and by mid-September thirty-nine of the forty-two delegates had signed the document. The next step sent the Constitution to the individual states for ratification. Opponents of the much larger and more powerful federal government created by the new Constitution became known as Antifederalists. Although they ultimately lost their cause with the adoption of the Constitution in 1789, their vociferous objections to the infringement on states' authority and the lack of protections for individual rights did not fade away but rather remained core issues in the evolution of American constitutionalism.

We the People of the United States, in Order to form a more perfect Union, establish Justice, insure domestic Tranquility, provide for the common defence, promote the general Welfare, and secure the Blessings of Liberty to ourselves and our Posterity, do ordain and establish this Constitution for the United States of America.

ARTICLE. I.

SECTION 1. All legislative Powers herein granted shall be vested in a Congress of the United States, which shall consist of a Senate and House of Representatives.

SECTION. 2. The House of Representatives shall be composed of Members chosen every second Year by the People of the several States, and the Electors in each State shall have the Qualifications requisite for Electors of the most numerous Branch of the State Legislature.

No Person shall be a Representative who shall not have attained to the Age of twenty five Years, and been seven Years a Citizen of the United States, and who shall not, when elected, be an Inhabitant of that State in which he shall be chosen.

Representatives and direct Taxes shall be apportioned among the several States which may be included within this Union, according to their respective Numbers, which shall be determined by adding to the whole Number of free Persons, including those bound to Service for a Term of Years, and excluding Indians not taxed, three fifths of all other Persons. The actual Enumeration shall be made within three Years after the first Meeting of the Congress of the United States, and within every subsequent Term of ten Years, in such Manner as they shall by Law direct. The Number of Representatives shall not exceed one for every thirty Thousand, but each State shall have at Least one Representative; and until such enumeration shall be made, the State of New Hampshire shall be entitled to chuse three, Massachusetts eight, Rhode-Island and Providence Plantations one, Connecticut five,

New-York six, New Jersey four, Pennsylvania eight, Delaware one, Maryland six, Virginia ten, North Carolina five, South Carolina five, and Georgia three.

When vacancies happen in the Representation from any State, the Executive Authority thereof shall issue Writs of Election to fill such Vacancies.

The House of Representatives shall chuse their Speaker and other Officers; and shall have the sole Power of Impeachment.

SECTION. 3. The Senate of the United States shall be composed of two Senators from each State, chosen by the Legislature thereof, for six Years; and each Senator shall have one Vote.

Immediately after they shall be assembled in Consequence of the first Election, they shall be divided as equally as may be into three Classes. The Seats of the Senators of the first Class shall be vacated at the Expiration of the second Year, of the second Class at the Expiration of the fourth Year, and of the third Class at the Expiration of the sixth Year, so that one third may be chosen every second Year; and if Vacancies happen by Resignation, or otherwise, during the Recess of the Legislature of any State, the Executive thereof may make temporary Appointments until the next Meeting of the Legislature, which shall then fill such Vacancies.

No Person shall be a Senator who shall not have attained to the Age of thirty Years, and been nine Years a Citizen of the United States, and who shall not, when elected, be an Inhabitant of that State for which he shall be chosen.

The Vice President of the United States shall be President of the Senate, but shall have no Vote, unless they be equally divided.

The Senate shall chuse their other Officers, and also a President pro tempore, in the Absence of the Vice President, or when he shall exercise the Office of President of the United States.

The Senate shall have the sole Power to try all Impeachments. When sitting for that Purpose, they shall be on Oath or Affirmation. When the President of the United States is tried, the Chief Justice shall preside: And no Person shall be convicted without the Concurrence of two thirds of the Members present.

Judgment in Cases of Impeachment shall not extend further than to removal from Office, and disqualification to hold and enjoy any Office of honor, Trust or Profit under the United States: but the Party convicted shall nevertheless be liable and subject to Indictment, Trial, Judgment and Punishment, according to Law.

SECTION. 4. The Times, Places and Manner of holding Elections for Senators and Representatives, shall be prescribed in each State by the Legislature thereof; but the Congress may at any time by Law make or alter such Regulations, except as to the Places of chusing Senators.

The Congress shall assemble at least once in every Year, and such Meeting shall be on the first Monday in December, unless they shall by Law appoint a different Day.

SECTION. 5. Each House shall be the Judge of the Elections, Returns and Qualifications of its own Members, and a Majority of each shall constitute a Quorum to do Business; but a smaller Number may adjourn from day to day, and may be authorized to compel the Attendance of absent Members, in such Manner, and under such Penalties as each House may provide.

Each House may determine the Rules of its Proceedings, punish its Members for disorderly Behaviour, and, with the Concurrence of two thirds, expel a Member.

Each House shall keep a Journal of its Proceedings, and from time to time publish the same, excepting such Parts as may in their Judgment require Secrecy; and the Yeas and Nays of the Members of either House on any question shall, at the Desire of one fifth of those Present, be entered on the Journal.

Neither House, during the Session of Congress, shall, without the Consent of the other, adjourn for more than three days, nor to any other Place than that in which the two Houses shall be sitting.

SECTION. 6. The Senators and Representatives shall receive a Compensation for their Services, to be ascertained by Law, and paid out of the Treasury of the United States. They shall in all Cases, except Treason, Felony and Breach of the Peace, be privileged from Arrest during their Attendance at the Session of their respective Houses, and in going to and returning from the same; and for any Speech or Debate in either House, they shall not be questioned in any other Place.

No Senator or Representative shall, during the Time for which he was elected, be appointed to any civil Office under the Authority of the United States, which shall have been created, or the Emoluments whereof shall have been encreased during such time; and no Person holding any Office under the United States, shall be a Member of either House during his Continuance in Office.

SECTION. 7. All Bills for raising Revenue shall originate in the House of Representatives; but the Senate may propose or concur with Amendments as on other Bills.

Every Bill which shall have passed the House of Representatives and the Senate, shall, before it become a Law, be presented to the President of the United States; If he approve he shall sign it, but if not he shall return it, with his Objections to that House in which it shall have originated, who shall enter the Objections at large on their Journal, and proceed to reconsider it. If after such Reconsideration two thirds of that House shall agree to pass the Bill, it shall be sent, together with the Objections, to the other House, by which it shall likewise be reconsidered, and if approved by two thirds of that House, it shall become a Law. But in all such Cases the Votes of both Houses shall be determined by yeas and Nays, and the Names of the Persons voting for and against the Bill shall be entered on the Journal of each House respectively. If any Bill shall not be returned by the President within ten Days (Sundays excepted) after it shall have been presented to him, the Same shall be a Law, in like Manner as if he had signed it, unless the Congress by their Adjournment prevent its Return, in which Case it shall not be a Law.

Every Order, Resolution, or Vote to which the Concurrence of the Senate and House of Representatives may be necessary (except on a question of Adjournment) shall be presented to the President of the United States; and before the Same shall take Effect, shall be approved by him, or being disapproved by him, shall be repassed by two thirds of the Senate and House of Representatives, according to the Rules and Limitations prescribed in the Case of a Bill.

SECTION. 8. The Congress shall have Power To lay and collect Taxes, Duties, Imposts and Excises, to pay the Debts and provide for the common Defence and general Welfare of the United States; but all Duties, Imposts and Excises shall be uniform throughout the United States;

To borrow Money on the credit of the United States;

To regulate Commerce with foreign Nations, and among the several States, and with the Indian Tribes;

To establish an uniform Rule of Naturalization, and uniform Laws on the subject of Bankruptcies throughout the United States;

To coin Money, regulate the Value thereof, and of foreign Coin, and fix the Standard of Weights and Measures;

To provide for the Punishment of counterfeiting the Securities and current Coin of the United States;

To establish Post Offices and post Roads;

To promote the Progress of Science and useful Arts, by securing for limited Times to Authors and Inventors the exclusive Right to their respective Writings and Discoveries;

To constitute Tribunals inferior to the Supreme Court;

To define and punish Piracies and Felonies committed on the high Seas, and Offences against the Law of Nations;

To declare War, grant Letters of Marque and Reprisal, and make Rules concerning Captures on Land and Water;

To raise and support Armies, but no Appropriation of Money to that Use shall be for a longer Term than two Years;

To provide and maintain a Navy;

To make Rules for the Government and Regulation of the land and naval Forces;

To provide for calling forth the Militia to execute the Laws of the Union, suppress Insurrections and repel Invasions;

To provide for organizing, arming, and disciplining, the Militia, and for governing such Part of them as may be employed in the Service of the United States, reserving to the States respectively, the Appointment of the Officers, and the Authority of training the Militia according to the discipline prescribed by Congress;

To exercise exclusive Legislation in all Cases whatsoever, over such District (not exceeding ten Miles square) as may, by Cession of particular States, and the Acceptance of Congress, become the Seat of the Government of the United States, and to exercise like Authority over all Places purchased by the Consent of the Legislature of the State in which the Same shall be, for the Erection of Forts, Magazines, Arsenals, dock-Yards, and other needful Buildings;—And

To make all Laws which shall be necessary and proper for carrying into Execution the foregoing Powers, and all other Powers vested by this Constitution in the Government of the United States, or in any Department or Officer thereof.

SECTION. 9. The Migration or Importation of such Persons as any of the States now existing shall think proper to admit, shall not be prohibited by the Congress prior to the Year one thousand eight hundred and eight, but a Tax or duty may be imposed on such Importation, not exceeding ten dollars for each Person.

The Privilege of the Writ of Habeas Corpus shall not be suspended, unless when in Cases of Rebellion or Invasion the public Safety may require it.

No Bill of Attainder or ex post facto Law shall be passed.

No Capitation, or other direct, Tax shall be laid, unless in Proportion to the Census or Enumeration herein before directed to be taken.

No Tax or Duty shall be laid on Articles exported from any State.

No Preference shall be given by any Regulation of Commerce or Revenue to the Ports of one State over those of another: nor shall Vessels bound to, or from, one State, be obliged to enter, clear, or pay Duties in another.

No Money shall be drawn from the Treasury, but in Consequence of Appropriations made by Law; and a regular Statement and Account of the Receipts and Expenditures of all public Money shall be published from time to time.

No Title of Nobility shall be granted by the United States: And no Person holding any Office of Profit or Trust under them, shall, without the Consent of the Congress, accept of any present, Emolument, Office, or Title, of any kind whatever, from any King, Prince, or foreign State.

SECTION. 10. No State shall enter into any Treaty, Alliance, or Confederation; grant Letters of Marque and Reprisal; coin Money; emit Bills of Credit; make any Thing but gold and silver Coin a Tender in Payment of Debts; pass any Bill of Attainder, ex post facto Law, or Law impairing the Obligation of Contracts, or grant any Title of Nobility.

No State shall, without the Consent of the Congress, lay any Imposts or Duties on Imports or Exports, except what may be absolutely necessary for executing its inspection Laws: and the net Produce of all Duties and Imposts, laid by any State on Imports or Exports, shall be for the Use of the Treasury of the United States; and all such Laws shall be subject to the Revision and Controul of the Congress.

No State shall, without the Consent of Congress, lay any Duty of Tonnage, keep Troops, or Ships of War in time of Peace, enter into any Agreement or Compact with another State, or with a foreign Power, or engage in War, unless actually invaded, or in such imminent Danger as will not admit of delay.

ARTICLE. II.

SECTION. 1. The executive Power shall be vested in a President of the United States of America. He shall hold his Office during the Term of four Years, and, together with the Vice President, chosen for the same Term, be elected, as follows

Each State shall appoint, in such Manner as the Legislature thereof may direct, a Number of Electors, equal to the whole Number of Senators and Representatives to which the State may be entitled in the Congress: but no Senator or Representative, or Person holding an Office of Trust or Profit under the United States, shall be appointed an Elector.

The Electors shall meet in their respective States, and vote by Ballot for two Persons, of whom one at least shall not be an Inhabitant of the same State with themselves. And they shall make a List of all the Persons voted for, and of the Number of Votes for each; which List they shall sign and certify, and transmit sealed to the Seat of the Government of the United States, directed to the President of the Senate. The President of the Senate shall, in the Presence of the Senate and House of Representatives, open all the Certificates, and the Votes shall then be counted. The Person having the greatest Number of Votes shall be the President, if such Number be a Majority of the whole Number of Electors appointed; and if there be more than one who have such Majority, and have an equal Number of Votes, then the House of Representatives shall immediately chuse by Ballot one of them for President; and if no Person have a Majority, then from the five highest on the List the said House shall in like Manner chuse the President. But in chusing the President, the Votes shall be taken by States, the Representation from each State having one Vote; A quorum for this Purpose shall consist of a Member or Members from two thirds of the States, and a Majority of all the States shall be necessary to a Choice. In every Case, after the Choice of the President, the Person having the greatest Number of Votes of the Electors shall be the Vice President. But if there should remain two or more who have equal Votes, the Senate shall chuse from them by Ballot the Vice President.

The Congress may determine the Time of chusing the Electors, and the Day on which they shall give their Votes; which Day shall be the same throughout the United States.

No Person except a natural born Citizen, or a Citizen of the United States, at the time of the Adoption of this Constitution, shall be eligible to the Office of President; neither shall any Person be eligible to that Office who shall not have attained to the Age of thirty five Years, and been fourteen Years a Resident within the United States.

In Case of the Removal of the President from Office, or of his Death, Resignation, or Inability to discharge the Powers and Duties of the said Office, the Same shall devolve on the Vice President, and the Congress may by Law provide for the Case of Removal, Death, Resignation or Inability, both of the President and Vice President, declaring what Officer shall then act as President, and such Officer shall act accordingly, until the Disability be removed, or a President shall be elected.

The President shall, at stated Times, receive for his Services, a Compensation, which shall neither be encreased nor diminished during the Period for which he shall have been elected, and he shall not receive within that Period any other Emolument from the United States, or any of them.

Before he enter on the Execution of his Office, he shall take the following Oath or Affirmation:—"I do solemnly swear (or affirm) that I will faithfully execute the Office of President of the United States, and will to the best of my Ability, preserve, protect and defend the Constitution of the United States."

SECTION. 2. The President shall be Commander in Chief of the Army and Navy of the United States, and of the Militia of the several States, when called into the actual Service of the United States; he may require the Opinion, in writing, of the principal Officer in each of the executive Departments, upon any Subject relating to the Duties of their respective Offices, and he shall have Power to grant Reprieves and Pardons for Offences against the United States, except in Cases of Impeachment.

He shall have Power, by and with the Advice and Consent of the Senate, to make Treaties, provided two thirds of the Senators present concur; and he shall nominate, and by and with the Advice and Consent of the Senate, shall appoint Ambassadors, other public Ministers and Consuls, Judges of the supreme Court, and all other Officers of the United States, whose Appointments are not herein otherwise provided for, and which shall be established by Law: but the Congress may by Law vest the Appointment of such inferior Officers, as they think proper, in the President alone, in the Courts of Law, or in the Heads of Departments.

The President shall have Power to fill up all Vacancies that may happen during the Recess of the Senate, by granting Commissions which shall expire at the End of their next Session.

SECTION. 3. He shall from time to time give to the Congress Information of the State of the Union, and recommend to their Consideration such Measures as he shall judge necessary and expedient; he may, on extraordinary Occasions, convene both Houses, or either of them, and in Case of Disagreement between them, with Respect to the Time of Adjournment, he may adjourn them to such Time as he shall think proper; he shall receive Ambassadors and other public Ministers; he shall take Care that the Laws be faithfully executed, and shall Commission all the Officers of the United States.

SECTION. 4. The President, Vice President and all civil Officers of the United States, shall be removed from Office on Impeachment for, and Conviction of, Treason, Bribery, or other high Crimes and Misdemeanors.

ARTICLE. III.

SECTION. 1. The judicial Power of the United States, shall be vested in one supreme Court, and in such inferior Courts as the Congress may from time to time ordain and establish. The Judges, both of the supreme and inferior Courts, shall hold their Offices during good Behaviour, and shall, at stated Times, receive for their Services, a Compensation, which shall not be diminished during their Continuance in Office.

SECTION. 2. The judicial Power shall extend to all Cases, in Law and Equity, arising under this Constitution, the Laws of the United States, and Treaties made, or which shall be made, under their Authority; — to all Cases affecting Ambassadors, other public Ministers and Consuls; — to all Cases of admiralty and maritime Jurisdiction; — to Controversies to which the United States shall be a Party; — to Controversies between two or more States; — between a State and Citizens of another State; — between Citizens of different States, — between Citizens of the same State claiming Lands under Grants of different States, and between a State, or the Citizens thereof, and foreign States, Citizens or Subjects.

In all Cases affecting Ambassadors, other public Ministers and Consuls, and those in which a State shall be Party, the supreme Court shall have original Jurisdiction. In all the other Cases before mentioned, the supreme Court shall have appellate Jurisdiction, both as to Law and Fact, with such Exceptions, and under such Regulations as the Congress shall make.

The Trial of all Crimes, except in Cases of Impeachment, shall be by Jury; and such Trial shall be held in the State where the said Crimes shall have been committed; but when not committed within any State, the Trial shall be at such Place or Places as the Congress may by Law have directed.

SECTION. 3. Treason against the United States, shall consist only in levying War against them, or in adhering to their Enemies, giving them Aid and Comfort. No Person shall be convicted of Treason unless on the Testimony of two Witnesses to the same overt Act, or on Confession in open Court.

The Congress shall have Power to declare the Punishment of Treason, but no Attainder of Treason shall work Corruption of Blood, or Forfeiture except during the Life of the Person attainted.

ARTICLE. IV.

SECTION. 1. Full Faith and Credit shall be given in each State to the public Acts, Records, and judicial Proceedings of every other State. And the Congress may by general Laws prescribe the Manner in which such Acts, Records and Proceedings shall be proved, and the Effect thereof.

SECTION. 2. The Citizens of each State shall be entitled to all Privileges and Immunities of Citizens in the several States.

A Person charged in any State with Treason, Felony, or other Crime, who shall flee from Justice, and be found in another State, shall on Demand of the executive Authority of the State from which he fled, be delivered up, to be removed to the State having Jurisdiction of the Crime.

No Person held to Service or Labour in one State, under the Laws thereof, escaping into another, shall, in Consequence of any Law or Regulation therein, be discharged from such Service or Labour, but shall be delivered up on Claim of the Party to whom such Service or Labour may be due.

SECTION. 3. New States may be admitted by the Congress into this Union; but no new State shall be formed or erected within the Jurisdiction of any other State; nor any State be formed by the Junction of two or more States, or Parts of States, without the Consent of the Legislatures of the States concerned as well as of the Congress.

The Congress shall have Power to dispose of and make all needful Rules and Regulations respecting the Territory or other Property belonging to the United States; and nothing in this Constitution shall be so construed as to Prejudice any Claims of the United States, or of any particular State.

SECTION. 4. The United States shall guarantee to every State in this Union a Republican Form of Government, and shall protect each of them against Invasion; and on Application of the Legislature, or of the Executive (when the Legislature cannot be convened) against domestic Violence.

ARTICLE. V.

The Congress, whenever two thirds of both Houses shall deem it necessary, shall propose Amendments to this Constitution, or, on the Application of the Legislatures of two thirds of the several States, shall call a Convention for proposing Amendments, which, in either Case, shall be valid to all Intents and Purposes, as Part of this Constitution, when ratified by the Legislatures of three fourths of the several States, or by Conventions in three fourths thereof, as the one or the other Mode of Ratification may be proposed by the Congress; Provided that no Amendment which may be made prior to the Year One thousand eight hundred and eight shall in any Manner affect the first and fourth Clauses in the Ninth

Section of the first Article; and that no State, without its Consent, shall be deprived of its equal Suffrage in the Senate.

ARTICLE. VI.

All Debts contracted and Engagements entered into, before the Adoption of this Constitution, shall be as valid against the United States under this Constitution, as under the Confederation.

This Constitution, and the Laws of the United States which shall be made in Pursuance thereof; and all Treaties made, or which shall be made, under the Authority of the United States, shall be the supreme Law of the Land; and the Judges in every State shall be bound thereby, any Thing in the Constitution or Laws of any State to the Contrary notwithstanding.

The Senators and Representatives before mentioned, and the Members of the several State Legislatures, and all executive and judicial Officers, both of the United States and of the several States, shall be bound by Oath or Affirmation, to support this Constitution; but no religious Test shall ever be required as a Qualification to any Office or public Trust under the United States.

ARTICLE. VII.

The Ratification of the Conventions of nine States, shall be sufficient for the Establishment of this Constitution between the States so ratifying the Same.

done in Convention by the Unanimous Consent of the States present the Seventeenth Day of September in the Year of our Lord one thousand seven hundred and Eighty seven and of the Independence of the United States of America the Twelfth In witness whereof We have hereunto subscribed our Names,

GO: WASHINGTON — Presidt. and deputy from Virginia

Source : Francis Newton Thorpe, ed., *The Federal and State Constitutions, Colonial Charters, and Other Organic Laws* (Washington, 1909), 1: 19–27.

The Federalist Papers (1787–1788)

When the delegates left Philadelphia, they had written the Constitution. Nonetheless, their work was hardly done. They had to go home and sell their work to the voters. The Constitution (in Article VII) said that "The ratification of the conventions of nine States shall be sufficient for the establishment of this Constitution." So, at least nine states had to ratify the proposed Constitution. In practical terms, this meant state elections to pick delegates to state ratifying conventions. Opponents of ratification came to be called Antifederalists; proponents, Federalists.

These names were misnomers. The Antifederalists believed in federalism — they wanted sovereign power distributed among the states. The Federalists wanted to shift power away from the states and to the national government. A better name for the Federalists would have been "Nationalists," but that is not the name they chose.

As the debate over ratifying the new Constitution continued, proponents faced a tough challenge in New York, which had taken advantage of the crucial economic importance of its harbor and profited through tariff and trade measures allowed under the Articles of Confederation. Leaders in New York, therefore, had little incentive to adopt the new Constitution. But one prominent New Yorker, Alexander Hamilton, proved forceful in leading a counter-offensive to convince New Yorkers of the new Constitution's merits. With James Madison and John Jay, Hamilton published a series of eighty-five essays explaining and defending the elements of the proposed constitution. Today, these essays document the fundamental principles of American constitutionalism.

The Federalist No. 10
James Madison

November 22, 1787

To the People of the State of New-York:
Among the numerous advantages promised by a well-constructed Union, none deserves to be more accurately devel-

oped than its tendency to break and control the violence of faction....

By a faction, I understand a number of citizens, whether amounting to a majority or minority of the whole, who are united and actuated by some common impulse of passion, or of interest, adverse to the rights of other citizens, or to the permanent and aggregate interests of the community.

There are two methods of curing the mischiefs of faction: the one, by removing its causes; the other, by controlling its effects....

It could never be more truly said than of the first remedy, that it was worse than the disease. Liberty is to faction what air is to fire, an aliment without which it instantly expires. But it could not be less folly to abolish liberty, which is essential to political life, because it nourishes faction, than it would be to wish the annihilation of air, which is essential to animal life, because it imparts to fire its destructive agency....

The inference to which we are brought is, that the *causes* of faction cannot be removed, and that relief is only to be sought in the means of controlling its *effects*.

If a faction consists of less than a majority, relief is supplied by the republican principle, which enables the majority to defeat its sinister views by regular vote: It may clog the administration, it may convulse the society; but it will be unable to execute and mask its violence under the forms of the Constitution. When a majority is included in a faction, the form of popular government on the other hand enables it to sacrifice to its ruling passion or interest both the public good and the rights of other citizens. To secure the public good and private rights against the danger of such a faction, and at the same time to preserve the spirit and the form of popular government, is then the great object to which our enquiries are directed: Let me add that it is the great desideratum, by which alone this form of government can be rescued from the opprobrium under which it has so long labored, and be recommended to the esteem and adoption of mankind....

The question resulting is, whether small or extensive Republics are most favorable to the election of proper guardians of the public weal; and it is clearly decided in favor of the latter by two obvious considerations:

In the first place it is to be remarked that however small the Republic may be, the representatives must be raised to a certain number, in order to guard against the cabals of a few; and that, however large it may be, they must be limited to a certain number, in order to guard against the confusion of a multitude. Hence the number of representatives in the two cases, not being in proportion to that of the Constituents, and being proportionally greatest in the small Republic, it follows, that if the proportion of fit characters, be not less, in the large than in the small Republic, the former will present a greater option, and consequently a greater probability of a fit choice.

In the next place, as each Representative will be chosen by a greater number of citizens in the large than in the small Republic, it will be more difficult for unworthy candidates to practice with success the vicious arts by which elections are too often carried; and the suffrages of the people being more free, will be more likely to center in men who possess the most attractive merit and the most diffusive and established characters.

It must be confessed, that in this, as in most other cases, there is a mean, on both sides of which inconveniences will be found to lie. By enlarging too much the number of electors, you render the representatives, too little acquainted with all their local circumstances and lesser interests; as by reducing it too much, you render him unduly attached to these, and too little fit to comprehend and pursue great and national objects. The Federal Constitution forms a happy combination in this respect; the great and aggregate interests being referred to the national, the local and particular, to the state legislatures.

The other point of difference is, the greater number of citizens and extent of territory which may be brought within the compass of Republican than of Democratic Government; and it is this circumstance principally which renders factious combinations less to be dreaded in the former, than in the latter. The smaller the society, the fewer probably will be the distinct parties and interests composing it; the fewer the distinct parties and interests, the more frequently will a majority be found of the same party; and the smaller the number of individuals composing a majority, and the smaller the compass within which they are placed, the more easily will they concert and execute their plans of oppression. Extend the sphere, and you take in a greater variety of parties and interests; you make it less probable that a majority of the whole will have a common motive to invade the rights of other citizens; or if such a common motive exists, it will be more difficult for all who feel it to discover their own strength, and to act in unison with each other. Besides other impediments, it may be remarked, that where there is a consciousness of unjust or dishonorable purposes, communication is always checked by distrust, in proportion to the number whose concurrence is necessary.

Hence, it clearly appears, that the same advantage which a Republic has over a Democracy, in controlling the effects of faction, is enjoyed by a large over a small Republic—is enjoyed by the Union over the States composing it. Does the advantage consist in the substitution of Representatives whose enlightened views and virtuous sentiments render them superior to local prejudices and schemes of injustice? It will not be denied that the Representation of the Union will most likely to possess these requisite endowments. Does it consist in the greater security afforded by a greater variety of parties, against the event of any one party being able to outnumber and oppress the rest? In an equal degree does the increased variety of parties comprised, within the Union, encrease this security. Does it, in fine, consist in the greater obstacles opposed to the concert and accomplishment of the secret wishes of an unjust and interested majority? Here, again, the extent of the Union gives it the most palpable advantage.

The influence of factious leaders may kindle a flame within their particular States, but will be unable to spread a general conflagration through the other States: a religious sect may degenerate into a political faction in a part of the Confederacy; but the variety of sects dispersed over the entire face of it, must secure the national Councils against any danger from that source: a rage for paper money, for an abolition of debts, for an equal division of property, or for any other improper or wicked project, will be less apt to pervade the whole body of the Union, than a particular member of it; in the same proportion as such a malady is more likely to taint a particular county or district, than an entire State....

Source: [New York] *The Daily Advertiser*, November 22, 1787.

The Federalist No. 39
James Madison

January 16, 1788

...But it was not sufficient, say the adversaries of the proposed Constitution, for the Convention to adhere to the republican form. They ought, with equal care, to have preserved the *federal* form, which regards the union as a *confederacy* of sovereign States; instead of which, they have framed a *national* government, which regards the union as a *consolidation* of the States. And it is asked by what authority this bold and radical innovation was undertaken. The handle which has been made of this objection requires, that it should be examined with some precision....

In order to ascertain the real character of the government it may be considered in relation to the foundation on which it is to be established; to the sources from which its ordinary powers are to be drawn; to the operation of those powers; to the extent of them; and to the authority by which future changes in the government are to be introduced.

On examining the first relation it appears on one hand, that the Constitution is to be founded on the assent and ratification of the people of America, given by deputies elected for the special purpose; but on the other that this assent and ratification is to be given by the people, not as individuals composing one entire nation, but as composing the distinct and independent States to which they respectively belong. It is to be the assent and ratification of the several States, derived from the supreme authority in each State, the authority of the people themselves. The act, therefore, establishing the Constitution, will not be a *national* but a *federal* act.

That it will be a federal and not a national act, as these terms are understood by the objectors, the act of the people as forming so many independent States, not as forming one aggregate nation, is obvious from this single consideration that it is to result neither from the decision of a *majority* of the people of the Union, nor from that of a *majority* of the States. It must result from the *unanimous* assent of the several States that are parties to it, differing no other wise from their ordinary assent than in its being expressed, not by the legislative authority, but by that of the people themselves. Were the people regarded in this transaction as forming one nation, the will of the majority of the whole people of the United States would bind the minority, in the same manner as the majority in each State must bind the minority; and the will of the majority must be determined either by a comparison of the individual votes; or by considering the will of the majority of the States, as evidence of the will of a majority of the people of the United States. Neither of these rules have been adopted. Each State, in ratifying the Constitution, is considered as a sovereign body, independent of all others, and only to be bound by its own voluntary act. In this relation, then, the new Constitution will, if established, be a *federal* and not a *national* constitution.

The next relation is, to the sources from which the ordinary powers of government are to be derived. The house of representatives will derive its powers from the people of America, and the people will be represented in the same proportion, and on the same principle, as they are in the legislature of a particular State. So far the Government is *national*, not *federal*. The Senate, on the other hand, will derive its powers from the States, as political and co-equal societies; and these will be represented on the principle of equality in the Senate, as they now are in the existing Congress. So far the government is *federal*, not *national*. The executive power will be derived from a very compound source. The immediate election of the President is to be made by the States in their political characters. The votes allotted to them, are in a compound ratio, which considers them partly as distinct and coequal societies;

partly as unequal members of the same society. The eventual election, again is to be made by that branch of the Legislature which consists of the national representatives; but in this particular act they are to be thrown into the form of individual delegations from so many distinct and co-equal bodies politic. From this aspect of the Government it appears to be of a mixed character, presenting at least as many *federal* as *national* features.

The difference between a federal and national Government, as it relates to the *operation of the government* is supposed to consist in this, that in the former the powers operate on the political bodies composing the confederacy, in their political capacities; in the latter, on the individual citizens composing the nation, in their individual capacities. On trying the Constitution by this criterion, it falls under the *national*, not the *federal* character; though perhaps not so completely as has been understood. In several cases, and particularly in the trial of controversies to which States may be parties, they must be viewed and proceeded against in their collective and political capacities only. So far the national countenance of the government on this side seems to be disfigured by a few federal features. But this blemish is perhaps unavoidable in any plan; and the operation of the government on the people, in their individual capacities, in its ordinary and most essential proceedings, may on the whole designate it in this relation a *national* government.

But if the government be national with regard to the *operation* of its powers, it changes its aspect again when we contemplate it in relation to the *extent* of its powers. The idea of a national government involves in it, not only an authority over the individual citizens; but an indefinite supremacy over all persons and things, so far as they are objects of lawful government. Among a people consolidated into one nation, this supremacy is completely vested in the national Legislature. Among communities united for particular purposes, it is vested partly in the general, and partly in the municipal Legislatures. In the former case, all local authorities are subordinate to the supreme; and may be controlled, directed, or abolished by it at pleasure. In the latter the local or municipal authorities form distinct and independent portions of the supremacy, no more subject within their respective spheres to the general authority, than the general authority is subject to them, within its own sphere. In this relation then the proposed Government cannot be deemed a *national* one; since its jurisdiction extends to certain enumerated objects only, and leaves to the several States a residuary and inviolable sovereignty over all other objects. It is true that in controversies relating to the boundary between the two jurisdictions, the tribunal which is ultimately to decide, is to be established under the general Government. But this does not change the principle of the case. The decision is to be impartially made, according to the rules of the Constitution; and all the usual and most effectual precautions are taken to secure this impartiality. Some such tribunal is clearly essential to prevent an appeal to the sword and a dissolution of the compact; and that it ought to be established under the general rather than under the local Governments, or, to speak more properly, that it could be safely established under the first alone, is a position not likely to be combated.

If we try the Constitution by its last relation, to the authority by which amendments are to be made, we find it neither wholly *national* nor wholly *federal*. Were it wholly national, the supreme and ultimate authority would reside in the *majority* of the people of the Union; and this authority would be competent at all times, like that of a majority of every national society, to alter or abolish its established Government. Were it wholly federal, on the other hand, the concurrence of each State in the Union would be essential to every alteration that would be binding on all. The mode provided by the plan of the Convention is not founded on either of these principles. In requiring more than a majority, and particularly, in computing the proportion by *States*, not by *citizens*, it departs from the *national* and advances towards the *federal* character; In rendering the concurrence of less than the whole number of States sufficient, it loses again the *federal* and partakes of the *national* character.

The proposed Constitution therefore is in strictness neither a national nor a federal Constitution; but a composition of both. In its foundation it is federal, not national; in the sources from which the ordinary powers of the Government are drawn, it is partly federal, and partly national: in the operation of these powers, it is national, not federal; in the extent of them again, it is federal, not national; And finally, in the authoritative mode of introducing amendments, it is neither wholly federal nor wholly national.

Source: [New York] *Independent Journal and the General Advertiser*, January 16, 1788.

The Federalist No. 51
James Madison

February 6, 1788

...the great security against a gradual concentration of the several powers in the same department, consists in giving to those who administer each department, the necessary constitutional means, and personal motives, to resist encroachments of the others. The provision for defense must in this, as in all other cases, be made commensurate to the danger of attack. Ambition must be made to counteract ambition. The interest of the man must be connected with the constitutional rights of the place. It may be a reflection on human nature, that such devices should be necessary to control the abuses of government. But what is government itself but the greatest of all reflections on human nature? If men were angels, no government would be necessary. If angels were to govern men, neither external nor internal controls on government would be necessary. In framing a government which is to be administered by men over men, the great difficulty lies in this: You must first enable the government to control the governed; and in the next place, oblige it to control itself. A dependence on the people is no doubt the primary control on the government; but experience has taught mankind the necessity of auxiliary precautions.

This policy of supplying, by opposite and rival interests, the defect of better motives, might be traced through the whole system of human affairs, private as well as public. We see it particularly displayed in all the subordinate distributions of power, where the constant aim is to divide and arrange the several offices in such a manner as that each may be a check on the other; that the private interest of every individual may be a sentinel over the public rights. These inventions of prudence cannot be less requisite in the distribution of the supreme powers of the State.

But it is not possible to give to each department an equal power of self defense. In republican government the legislative authority, necessarily, predominates. The remedy for this inconveniency is, to divide the legislature into different branches; and to render them, by different modes of election, and different principles of action, as little connected with each other as the nature of their common functions, and their common dependence on the society, will admit. It may even be necessary to guard against dangerous encroachments by still further precautions. As the weight of the legislative authority requires that it should be thus divided, the weakness of the executive may require, on the other hand, that it should be fortified. An absolute negative, on the legislature, appears at first view to be the natural defense with which the executive magistrate should be armed. But perhaps it would be neither altogether safe, nor alone sufficient. On ordinary occasions, it might not be exerted with the requisite firmness; and on extraordinary occasions it might be perfidiously abused. May not this defect of an absolute negative be supplied, by some qualified connection between this weaker department, and the weaker branch of the stronger department, by which the latter may be led to support the constitutional rights of the former, without being too much detached from the rights of its own department?

If the principles on which these observations are founded be just, as I persuade myself they are, and they be applied as a criterion, to the several State constitutions, and to the federal constitution, it will be found, that if the latter does not perfectly correspond with them, the former are infinitely less able to bear such a test....

Source: [New York] *Independent Journal and the General Advertiser*, February 6, 1788.

The Federalist No. 78
Alexander Hamilton

1788

...Whoever attentively considers the different departments of power must perceive, that, in a government in which they are separated from each other, the judiciary, from the nature of its functions, will always be the least dangerous to the political rights of the Constitution; because it will be least in a capacity to annoy or injure them. The Executive not only dispenses the honors, but holds the sword of the community. The legislature not only commands the purse, but prescribes the rules by which the duties and rights of every citizen are to be regulated. The judiciary, on the contrary, has no influence over either the sword or the purse; no direction either of the strength or of the wealth of the society; and can take no active resolution whatever. It may truly be said to have neither FORCE nor WILL, but merely judgment; and must ultimately depend upon the aid of the executive arm even for the efficacy of its judgments.

This simple view of the matter suggests several important consequences. It proves incontestably, that the judiciary is beyond comparison the weakest of the three departments of power; that it can never attack with success either of the other two; and that all possible care is requisite to enable it to defend itself against their attacks. It equally proves, that though individual oppression may now and then proceed from the courts of justice, the general liberty of the people can never be endangered from that quarter; I mean so long as the judiciary remains truly distinct from both the legislature and the Executive. For I agree, that ``there is no liberty, if the power of judging be not separated from the legislative and executive powers.'' And it proves, in the last place, that as liberty can have nothing to fear from the judiciary alone, but would have every thing to fear from its union with either of the other departments; that as all the effects of such a union must ensue from a dependence of the former on the latter, notwithstanding a nominal and apparent separation; that as, from the natural feebleness of the judiciary, it is in continual jeopardy of being overpowered, awed, or influenced by its co-ordinate branches; and that as nothing can contribute so much to its firmness and independence as permanency in office, this quality may therefore be justly regarded as an indispensable ingredient in its constitution, and, in a great measure, as the citadel of the public justice and the public security.

The complete independence of the courts of justice is peculiarly essential in a limited Constitution. By a limited Constitution, I understand one which contains certain specified exceptions to the legislative authority; such, for instance, as that it shall pass no bills of attainder, no ex-post-facto laws, and the like. Limitations of this kind can be preserved in practice no other way than through the medium of courts of justice, whose duty it must be to declare all acts contrary to the manifest tenor of the Constitution void. Without this, all the reservations of particular rights or privileges would amount to nothing.

Some perplexity respecting the rights of the courts to pronounce legislative acts void, because contrary to the Constitution, has arisen from an imagination that the doctrine would imply a superiority of the judiciary to the legislative power. It is urged that the authority which can declare the acts of another void, must necessarily be superior to the one whose acts may be declared void. As this doctrine is of great importance in all the American constitutions, a brief discussion of the ground on which it rests cannot be unacceptable.

There is no position which depends on clearer principles, than that every act of a delegated authority, contrary to the tenor of the commission under which it is exercised, is void. No legislative act, therefore, contrary to the Constitution, can be valid. To deny this, would be to affirm, that the deputy is greater than his principal; that the servant is above his master; that the representatives of the people are superior to the people themselves; that men acting by virtue of powers, may do not only what their powers do not authorize, but what they forbid.

If it be said that the legislative body are themselves the constitutional judges of their own powers, and that the construction they put upon them is conclusive upon the other departments, it may be answered, that this cannot be the natural presumption, where it is not to be collected from any particular provisions in the Constitution. It is not otherwise to be supposed, that the Constitution could intend to enable the representatives of the people to substitute their WILL to that of their constituents. It is far more rational to suppose, that the courts were designed to be an intermediate body between the people and the legislature, in order, among other things, to keep the latter within the limits assigned to their authority. The interpretation of the laws is the proper and peculiar province of the courts. A constitution is, in fact, and must be regarded by the judges, as a fundamental law. It therefore belongs to them to ascertain its meaning, as well as the meaning of any particular act proceeding from the legislative body. If there should happen to be an irreconcilable variance between the two, that which has the superior obligation and validity ought, of course, to be preferred; or, in other words, the Constitution ought to be preferred to the statute, the intention of the people to the intention of their agents.

Nor does this conclusion by any means suppose a superiority of the judicial to the legislative power. It only supposes that the power of the people is superior to both; and that where the will of the legislature, declared in its statutes, stands in opposition to that of the people, declared in the Constitution, the judges ought to be governed by the latter rather than the former. They ought to regulate their decisions by the fundamental laws, rather than by those which are not fundamental....

Source: Paul Leicester Ford, *The Federalist: A Commentary on the Constitution of the United States* (New York, 1898), 518–522.

Essay on the Constitution (1787)
"Brutus"

While a number of Antifederalists wrote in opposition to the new constitution, a writer calling himself "Brutus" proved the most articulate and effective. The actual identity of "Brutus" remains a mystery, but his essays appeared in the

New York Journal *between October 1787 and April 1788. Brutus and the Antifederalists remained true to the small-state ideals prevalent at the beginning of the Revolution. They disputed the notion that the new nation's serious problems would be rectified by instituting a stronger and more powerful national government. In their view, the only true republics were small.*

Brutus No. 1

October 18, 1787

...History furnishes no example of a free republic, any thing like the extent of the United States. The Grecian republics were of small extent; so also was that of the Romans. Both of these, it is true, in process of time, extended their conquests over large territories of country; and the consequence was, that their governments were changed from that of free governments to those of the most tyrannical that ever existed in the world.

Not only the opinion of the greatest men, and the experience of mankind, are against the idea of an extensive republic, but a variety of reasons may be drawn from the reason and nature of things, against it. In every government, the will of the sovereign is the law. In despotic governments, the supreme authority being lodged in one, his will is law, and can be as easily expressed to a large extensive territory as to a small one. In a pure democracy the people are the sovereign, and their will is declared by themselves; for this purpose they must all come together to deliberate, and decide. This kind of government cannot be exercised, therefore, over a country of any considerable extent; it must be confined to a single city, or at least limited to such bounds as that the people can conveniently assemble, be able to debate, understand the subject submitted to them, and declare their opinion concerning it.

In a free republic, although all laws are derived from the consent of the people, yet the people do not declare their consent by themselves in person, but by representatives, chosen by them, who are supposed to know the minds of their constituents, and to be possessed of integrity to declare this mind.

In every free government, the people must give their assent to the laws by which they are governed. This is the true criterion between free government and an arbitrary one. The former are ruled by the will of the whole, expressed in any manner they may agree upon; the latter by the will of one, or a few. If the people are to give their assent to the laws, by persons chosen and appointed by them, the manner of the choice and the number chosen, must be such, as to possess, be disposed, and consequently qualified to declare the sentiments of the people; for if they do not know, or are not disposed to speak the sentiments of the people, the people do not govern, but the sovereignty is in a few. Now, in a large extended country, it is impossible to have a representation, possessing the sentiments, and of integrity, to declare the minds of the people, without having it so numerous and unwieldly, as to be subject in great measure to the inconveniency of a democratic government.

The territory of the United States is of vast extent; it now contains near three millions of souls, and is capable of containing much more than ten times that number. Is it practicable for a country, so large and so numerous as they will soon become, to elect a representation, that will speak their sentiments, without their becoming so numerous as to be incapable of transacting public business? It certainly is not.

In a republic, the manners, sentiments, and interests of the people should be similar. If this be not the case, there will be a constant clashing of opinions; and the representatives of one part will be continually striving against those of the other. This will retard the operations of government, and prevent such conclusions as will promote the public good. If we apply this remark to the condition of the United States, we shall be convinced that it forbids that we should be one government. The United States includes a variety of climates. The productions of the different parts of the union are very variant, and their interests, of consequence, diverse. Their manners and habits differ as much as their climates and productions; and their sentiments are by no means coincident. The laws and customs of the several states are, in many respects, very diverse, and in some opposite; each would be in favor of its own interests and customs, and, of consequence, a legislature, formed of representatives from the respective parts, would not only be too numerous to act with any care or decision, but would be composed of such heterogenous and discordant principles, as would constantly be contending with each other.

...A free republic will never keep a standing army to execute its laws. It must depend upon the support of its citizens. But when a government is to receive its support from the aid of the citizens, it must be so constructed as to have the confidence, respect, and affection of the people. Men who, upon the call of the magistrate, offer themselves to execute the laws, are influenced to do it either by affection to the government, or from fear; where a standing army is at hand to punish offenders, every man is actuated by the latter principle, and therefore, when the magistrate calls, will obey: but, where this is not the case, the government must rest for its support upon the confidence and respect which the people have for their government and laws. The body of the people being attached, the government will always be sufficient to support and execute its laws, and to operate upon the fears of any faction which may be opposed to it, not only to prevent an opposition to the execution of the laws themselves, but also to compel the most of them to aid the magistrate; but the people will not be likely to have such confidence in their rulers, in a republic so extensive as the United States, as necessary for these purposes. The confidence which the people have in their rulers, in a free republic, arises from their knowing them, from their being responsible to them for their conduct, and from the power they have of displacing them when they misbehave: but in a republic of the extent of this continent, the people in general would be acquainted with very few of their rulers: the people at large would know little of their proceedings, and it would be extremely difficult to change them. The people in Georgia and New Hampshire would not know one another's mind, and therefore could not act in concert to enable them to effect a general change of representatives. The different parts of so extensive a country could not possibly be made acquainted with the conduct of their representatives, nor be informed of the reasons upon which measures were founded. The consequence will be, they will have no confidence in their legislature, suspect them of ambitious views, be jealous of every measure they adopt, and will not support the laws they pass. Hence the government will be nerveless and inefficient, and no way will be left to render it otherwise, but by establishing an armed force to execute the laws at the point of the bayonet—a government of all others the most to be dreaded.

In a republic of such vast extent as the United-States, the legislature cannot attend to the various concerns and wants of its different parts. It cannot be sufficiently numerous to be acquainted with the local condition and wants of the different districts, and if it could, it is impossible it should have sufficient time to attend to and provide for all the variety of cases of this nature, that would be continually arising.

In so extensive a republic, the great officers of government would soon become above the controul of the people, and abuse their power to the purpose of aggrandizing themselves, and oppressing them. The trust committed to the executive offices, in a country of the extent of the United States, must be various and of magnitude. The command of all the troops and navy of the republic, the appointment of officers, the power of pardoning offences, the collecting of all the public revenues, and the power of expending them, with a number of other powers, must be lodged and exercised in every state, in the hands of a few. When these are attended with great honor and emolument, as they always will be in large states, so as greatly to interest men to pursue them, and to be proper objects for ambitious and designing men, such men will be ever restless in their pursuit after them. They will use the power, when they have acquired it, to the purposes of gratifying their own interest and ambition, and it is scarcely possible, in a very large republic, to call them to account for their misconduct, or to prevent their abuse of power.

These are some of the reasons by which it appears, that a free republic cannot long subsist over a country of the great extent of these states. If then this new constitution is calculated to consolidate the thirteen states into one, as it evidently is, it ought not to be adopted....

Source: *New York Journal*, October 18, 1787.

Brutus No. 6

27 December 1787

It is an important question, whether the general government of the United States should be so framed, as to absorb and swallow up the state governments? or whether, on the contrary, the former ought not to be confined to certain defined national objects, while the latter should retain all the powers which concern the internal police of the states?

I have, in my former papers, offered a variety of arguments to prove, that a simple free government could not be exercised over this whole continent, and that therefore we must either give up our liberties and submit to an arbitrary one, or frame a constitution on the plan of confederation. Further reasons might be urged to prove this point—but it seems unnecessary, because the principal advocates of the new constitution admit of the position. The question therefore between us, this being admitted, is, whether or not this system is so formed as either directly to annihilate the state governments, or that in its operation it will certainly effect it. If this is answered in the affirmative, then the system ought not to be adopted, without such amendments as will avoid this consequence. If on the contrary it can be shewn, that the state governments are secured in their rights to manage the internal police of the respective states, we must confine ourselves in our enquiries to the organization of the government and the guards and provisions it contains to prevent a misuse or abuse of power. To determine this question, it is requisite, that we fully investigate the nature, and the extent of the powers intended to be granted by this constitution to the rulers.

...The general government is to be vested with authority to levy and collect taxes, duties, and excises; the separate states have also power to impose taxes, duties, and excises, except that they cannot lay duties on exports and imports without the consent of Congress. Here then the two governments have concurrent jurisdiction; both may lay impositions of this kind. But then the general government have supperadded to this power, authority to make all laws which shall be necessary and proper for carrying the foregoing power into execution. Suppose then that both governments should lay taxes, duties, and excises, and it should fall so heavy on the people that they would be unable, or be so burdensome that they would refuse to pay them both — would it not be necessary that the general legislature should suspend the collection of the state tax? It certainly would. For, if the people could not, or would not pay both, they must be discharged from the tax to the state, or the tax to the general government could not be collected. — The conclusion therefore is inevitable, that the respective state governments will not have the power to raise one shilling in any way, but by the permission of the Congress. I presume no one will pretend, that the states can exercise legislative authority, or administer justice among their citizens for any length of time, without being able to raise a sufficiency to pay those who administer their governments.

If this be true, and if the states can raise money only by permission of the general government, it follows that the state governments will be dependent on the will of the general government for their existence....

Source: *New York Journal*, December 27, 1787.

Brutus No. 12

14 February 1788

...I proceed, 2d, To inquire, in what manner this power will increase the jurisdiction of the courts...[T]his power will diminish and destroy both the legislative and judicial authority of the states.

It is obvious that these courts will have authority to decide upon the validity of the laws of any of the states, in all cases where they come in question before them. Where the constitution gives the general government exclusive jurisdiction, they will adjudge all laws made by the states, in such cases, void.... Where the constitution gives them concurrent jurisdiction, the laws of the United States must prevail, because they are the supreme law. In such cases, therefore, the laws of the state legislatures must be repealed, restricted, or so construed, as to give full effect to the laws of the union on the same subject. From these remarks it is easy to see, that in proportion as the general government acquires power and jurisdiction, by the liberal construction which the judges may give the constitution, will those of the states lose its rights, until they become so trifling and unimportant, as not to be worth having....

Source: *New York Journal*, February 14, 1788.

The Bill of Rights (1791)

A promise to include specifically enumerated provisions protecting individual rights proved crucial to the ratification of the United States Constitution, and the new national legislature moved quickly to add ten amendments to fulfill this promise. The "Bill of Rights" was historically unprecedented. While the notion of individual rights had ancient roots in many legal systems, no other government had ever provided a written list of protections for citizens' liberties. Along with the evolution of federalism, the guarantees included in the Bill of Rights for all American citizens would become the most important story in the history of American constitutionalism. The story is still unfolding to this day.

Amendment I. Congress shall make no law respecting an establishment of religion, or prohibiting the free exercise thereof; or abridging the freedom of speech, or of the press; or the right of the people peaceably to assemble, and to petition the Government for a redress of grievances.

Amendment II. A well regulated Militia, being necessary to the security of a free State, the right of the people to keep and bear Arms, shall not be infringed.

Amendment III. No Soldier shall, in time of peace be quartered in any house, without the consent of the Owner, nor in time of war, but in a manner to be prescribed by law.

Amendment IV. The right of the people to be secure in their persons, houses, papers, and effects, against unreasonable searches and seizures, shall not be violated, and no Warrants shall issue, but upon probable cause, supported by Oath or affirmation, and particularly describing the place to be searched, and the persons or things to be seized.

Amendment V. No person shall be held to answer for a capital, or otherwise infamous crime, unless on a presentment or indictment of a Grand Jury, except in cases arising in the land or naval forces, or in the Militia, when in actual service in time of War or public danger; nor shall any person be subject for the same offence to be twice put in jeopardy of life or limb; nor shall be compelled in any criminal case to be a witness against himself, nor be deprived of life, liberty, or property, without due process of law; nor shall private property be taken for public use, without just compensation.

Amendment VI. In all criminal prosecutions, the accused shall enjoy the right to a speedy and public trial, by an impartial jury of the State and district wherein the crime shall have been committed, which district shall have been previously ascertained by law, and to be informed of the nature and cause of the accusation; to be confronted with the witnesses against him; to have compulsory process for obtaining witnesses in his favor, and to have the Assistance of Counsel for his defence.

Amendment VII. In Suits at common law, where the value in controversy shall exceed twenty dollars, the right of trial by jury shall be preserved, and no fact tried by a jury, shall be otherwise reexamined in any Court of the United States, than according to the rules of the common law.

Amendment VIII. Excessive bail shall not be required, nor excessive fines imposed, nor cruel and unusual punishments inflicted.

Amendment IX. The enumeration in the Constitution, of certain rights, shall not be construed to deny or disparage others retained by the people.

Amendment X. The powers not delegated to the United States by the Constitution, nor prohibited by it to the States, are reserved to the States respectively, or to the people.

Source: Francis Newton Thorpe, ed., *The Federal and State Constitutions, Colonial Charters, and other Organic Laws* (Washington, 1909), 1:29–30.

5.

The Early American Republic

With the ratification of the Constitution in 1789, the new republic had established a basic framework for government and law. But tensions between the states and the new national authority continued and, in fact, became the heart of the debate of how to interpret the Constitution's broad language. Americans soon found themselves enmeshed in heated debate over whether the powers the Constitution granted to the federal government were to be interpreted strictly, reining in the government's actions, or more broadly, allowing it greater authority to actively address problems confronting the nation.

The debate over the extent of the national government's power reflected differing visions for the new nation's future. Some believed the republic should remain a primarily agrarian society governed through diffuse centers of power. For these Americans, the powers the Constitution granted to the federal government were to be interpreted narrowly, leaving the most significant portion of authority to the individual states. Others, however, envisioned an emerging industrial giant directed more effectively and efficiently by a strong central government. These competing ideologies formed the basis for the first American political parties, the Federalists and the Republicans. But the rise of political partisanship was a development not accounted for in the Constitution. Indeed, many Revolutionary leaders—including President George Washington—decried what they saw as the threat to the new nation's stability posed by the existence of warring factions. Making the Revolution's goal of government by the people into a workable reality proved to be an arduous task. Many of the arguments about how to make federalism work that were raised in the republic's difficult early years have persisted in various forms throughout American history.

Federal Judiciary Act (1789)

Article III of the Constitution established the judiciary as the third branch of the federal government. But while it vested power in the United States Supreme Court, the document was otherwise quite vague on the function of inferior courts within the federal judiciary. Federalists and Republicans debated the reach of the federal courts and the extent to which state courts would retain their authority. The system finally established by Congress in the Judiciary Act of 1789 provided a compromise between the two positions, allowing state courts concurrent jurisdiction with the new federal courts where federal laws were concerned.

An Act to Establish the Judicial Courts of the United States.

SECTION 1. *Be it enacted by the Senate and House of Representatives of the United States of America in Congress assembled,* That the supreme court of the United States shall consist of a chief justice and five associate justices, any four of whom shall be a quorum, and shall hold annually at the seat of government two sessions, the one commencing the first Monday of February, and the other the first Monday of August. That the associate justices shall have precedence according to the date of their commissions, or when the commissions of two or more of them bear date on the same day, according to their respective ages....

SECT. 3. *And be it further enacted,* That there be a court called a District Court, in each of the afore mentioned districts, to consist of one judge, who shall reside in the district for which he is appointed, and shall be called a District Judge....

SECT. 8. *And be it further enacted,* That the justices of the Supreme Court, and the district judges, before they proceed to execute the duties of their respective offices, shall take the following oath or affirmation, to wit: "I, A. B., do solemnly swear or affirm, that I will administer justice without respect to persons, and do equal right to the poor and to the rich, and that I will faithfully and impartially discharge and perform all the duties incumbent on me as_____, according to the best of my abilities and understanding, agreeably to the constitution and laws of the United States. So help me God."

SECT. 9. *And be it further enacted,* That the district courts shall have, exclusively of the courts of the several States, cognizance of all crimes and offences that shall be cognizable under the authority of the United States, committed within their respective districts, or upon the high seas; where no other punishment than whipping, not exceeding thirty stripes, a fine not exceeding one hundred dollars, or a term of imprisonment not exceeding six months, is to be inflicted; and shall also have exclusive original cognizance of all civil causes of admiralty and maritime jurisdiction, including all seizures under laws of impost, navigation or trade of the United States, where the seizures are made, on waters which are navigable from the sea by vessels of ten or more tons burthen, within their respective districts as well as upon the high seas; saving to suitors, in all cases, the right of a common law remedy, where the common law is competent to give it; and shall also have exclusive original cognizance of all seizures on land, or other waters than as aforesaid, made, and of all suits for penalties and forfeitures incurred, under the laws of the United States. And shall also have cognizance, concurrent with the courts of the several States, or the circuit courts, as the case may be, of all causes where an alien sues for a tort only in violation of the law of nations or a treaty of the United States. And shall also have cognizance, concurrent as last mentioned, of all suits at common law where the United States sue, and the matter in dispute amounts, exclusive of costs, to the sum or value of one hundred dollars. And shall also have jurisdiction exclusively of the courts of the several States, of all suits against consuls or vice-consuls, except for offences above the description aforesaid. And the trial of issues in fact, in the district courts, in all causes except civil causes of admiralty and maritime jurisdiction, shall be by jury....

SECT. 11. *And be it further enacted,* That the circuit courts shall have original cognizance, concurrent with the course of the several States, of all suits of a civil nature at common law or in equity, where the matter in dispute exceeds, exclusive of costs, the sum or value of five hundred dollars, and the United States are plaintiffs, or petitioners; or an alien is a party, or the suit is between a citizen of the State where the suit is brought, and a citizen of another State. And shall have exclusive cognizance of all crimes and offences cognizable under the authority of the United States, except where this act otherwise provides, or the laws of the United States shall otherwise direct, and concurrent jurisdiction with the district courts of the crimes and offences cognizable therein. But no person shall be arrested in one district for trial in another, in any civil action before a circuit or district court. And no civil suit shall be brought before either of said courts against an inhabitant of the United States, by any original process in any other district than that whereof he is an inhabitant, or in which he shall be found at the time of serving the writ, nor shall any district or circuit court have cognizance of any suit to recover the contents of any promissory note or other chose in action in favour of an assignee, unless a suit might have been prosecuted in such court to recover the said contents if no assignment had been made, except in cases of foreign bills of exchange. And the circuit courts shall also have appellate jurisdiction from the district courts under the regulations and restrictions herein after provided....

SECT. 13. *And be it further enacted,* That the Supreme Court shall have exclusive jurisdiction of all controversies of a civil nature, where a state is a party, except between a state and its citizens; and except also between a state and citizens of other states, or aliens, in which latter case it shall have original but not exclusive jurisdiction. And shall have exclusively all such jurisdiction of suits or proceedings against ambassadors, or other public ministers, or their domestics, or domestic servants, as a court of law can have or exercise consistently with the law of nations; and original, but not exclusive jurisdiction of all suits brought by ambassadors, or other public ministers, or in which a consul, or vice consul, shall be a party. And the trial of issues in fact in the Supreme Court, in all actions at law against citizens of the United States, shall be by jury. The Supreme Court shall also have appellate jurisdiction from the circuit courts and courts of the several states, in the cases herein after specially provided for; and shall have power to issue writs of prohibition to the district courts, when proceeding as courts of admiralty and maritime jurisdiction, and writs of mandamus, in cases warranted by the principles and usages of law, to any courts appointed, or persons holding office, under the authority of the United States.

SECT. 14. *And be it further enacted,* That all the before-mentioned courts of the United States, shall have power to issue writs of *scire facias, habeas corpus,* and all other writs not specially provided for by statute, which may be necessary for the exercise of their respective jurisdictions, and agreeable to the principles and usages of law. And that either of the justices of the supreme court, as well as judges of the district courts, shall have power to grant writs of habeas corpus for the purpose of an inquiry into the cause of commitment. --*Provided,* That writs of habeas corpus shall in no case extend to prisoners in gaol, unless where they are in custody, under or by colour of the authority of the United States, or are committed for trial before some court of the same, or are necessary to be brought into court to testify....

SECT. 17. *And be it further enacted,* That all the said courts of the United States shall have power to grant new trials, in cases where there has been a trial by jury for reasons for which new trials have usually been granted in the courts of law; and shall have power to impose and administer all necessary oaths or affirmations, and to punish by fine or imprisonment, at the discretion of said courts, all contempts of authority in any cause or hearing before the same; and to make and establish all necessary rules for the orderly conducting [of] business in the said courts, provided such rules are not repugnant to the laws of the United States....

SECT. 35. *That in all the courts of the United States,* the parties may plead and manage their own causes personally or by the assistance of such counselor attorneys at law as by the rules of the said courts respectively shall be permitted to manage and conduct causes therein. And there shall be appointed in each district a meet person learned in the law to act as attorney for the United States in such district who shall be sworn or affirmed to the faithful execution of his office, whose duty it shall be to prosecute in such district all delinquents for crimes and offences, cognizable under the authority of the United States, and all civil actions in which the United States shall be concerned, except before the supreme court in the district in which that court shall be holden. And he shall receive as a compensation for his services such fees as shall be taxed therefor in the respective courts before which the suits or prosecutions shall be. And there shall also be appointed a meet person, learned in the law, to act as attorney-general for the United States, who shall be sworn or affirmed to a faithful execution of his office; whose duty shall it be to prosecute and conduct all suits in the Supreme Court in which the United States shall be concerned, and to give his advice and opinion upon questions of law when required by the President of the United States, or when requested by the heads of any of the departments, touching any matters that may concern their departments, and shall receive such compensation for his services as shall by law be provided.

Approved, September 24, 1789.

Source: Richard Peters, ed., *Public Statutes at Large of the United States of America* (Boston, 1845), 1:73–74, 76–77, 78 – 79, 80– 82, 83, 92– 93.

Jefferson and Hamilton Debate the Bank of the United States (1791)

In 1790, Secretary of the Treasury Alexander Hamilton offered Congress his plan for servicing the fifty million dollar national debt. As a device for expanding the national sovereignty, Hamilton proposed that the national government take over the states' debts. This meant asking all taxpayers to pay off the debts of the states. Since the northern states owed more than the southern states, southerners, including Hamilton's erstwhile ally James Madison, objected.

Hamilton and Madison worked out their differences over dinner. Madison agreed to use his influence among southern congressmen for Hamilton's proposal if Hamilton used his influence among New Englanders to permanently locate the capitol on the Potomac rather than in Philadelphia. The capitol would temporarily stay in Philadelphia for ten years but then move to a spot between Maryland and Virginia, two southern states.

At first the deal seemed to have smoothed over resistance to Hamilton's nationalism. But then Pennsylvania's congressional delegation, realizing the enormity of their state's loss if the capitol went south, raised objections. The Pennsylvania legislature appropriated money to build a permanent capitol building in Philadelphia. At this point, what had been a tangential element in the Hamilton plan became the central issue. As a part of his nationalist plan, Hamilton wanted to centralize control of the nation's money in a central bank. And Hamilton had planned to locate the headquarters of his bank not on the Potomac, but in Philadelphia. Hamilton's proposed bank would have a charter for twenty years, not ten. To southerners, the bank's Philadelphia home seemed to symbolize northern duplicity. Southerners asked if their northern friends could really be trusted to move the capitol once they had achieved what they really wanted, an overly powerful national government.

At this point, Secretary of State Thomas Jefferson, heretofore silent, strongly objected to Hamilton's bank proposal, arguing the Republican view that the creation of a national bank lay far outside the boundaries the Constitution set on federal power. George Washington asked the advice of both Hamilton and Jefferson. Examining their replies today provides a clear elucidation of the Federalist and Republican positions on strict versus broad interpretations of constitutional power.

Opinion on the Constitutionality of a National Bank
Thomas Jefferson

February 15, 1791

...I consider the foundation of the Constitution as laid on this ground: That "all powers not delegated to the United States, by the Constitution, nor prohibited by it to the States, are reserved to the States or to the people." To take a single step beyond the boundaries thus specially drawn around the powers of Congress, is to take possession of a boundless field of power, no longer susceptible of any definition.

The incorporation of a bank, and the powers assumed by this bill, have not, in my opinion, been delegated to the United States, by the Constitution.

I. They are not among the powers specially enumerated: for these are: Ist. A power to lay taxes for the purpose of paying the debts of the United States; but no debt is paid by this bill, nor any tax laid. Were it a bill to raise money, its origination in the Senate would condemn it by the Constitution.

2. "To borrow money." But this bill neither borrows money nor ensures the borrowing it. The proprietors of the bank will be just as free as any other money holders, to lend or not to lend their money to the public. The operation proposed in the bill, first, to lend them two millions, and then to borrow them back again, cannot change the nature of the latter act, which will still be a payment, and not a loan, call it by what name you please.

3. To "regulate commerce with foreign nations, and among the States, and with the Indian tribes." To erect a bank, and to regulate commerce, are very different acts. He who erects a bank, creates a subject of commerce in its bills; so does he who makes a bushel of wheat, or digs a dollar out of the mines; yet neither of these persons regulates commerce thereby. To make a thing which may be bought and sold, is not to prescribe regulations for buying and selling. Besides, if this was an exercise of the power of regulating commerce, it would be void, as extending as much to the internal commerce of every State, as to its external. For the power given to Congress by the Constitution does not extend to the internal regulation of the commerce of a State, (that is to say of the commerce between citizen and citizen,) which remain exclusively with its own legislature; but to its external commerce only, that is to say, its commerce with another State, or with foreign nations, or with the Indian tribes. Accordingly the bill does not propose the measure as a regulation of trade, but as "productive of considerable advantages to trade." Still less are these powers covered by any other of the special enumerations.

II. Nor are they within either of the general phrases, which are the two following:

1. To lay taxes to provide for the general welfare of the United States, that is to say, "to lay taxes for *the purpose* of providing for the general welfare." For the laying of taxes is the *power*, and the general welfare the *purpose* for which the power is to be exercised. They are not to lay taxes *ad libitum for any purpose they please*; but only *to pay the debts or provide for the welfare of the Union*. In like manner, they are not *to do anything they please* to provide for the general welfare, but only to *lay taxes* for that purpose. To consider the latter phrase, not as describing the purpose of the first, but as

giving a distinct and independent power to do any act they please, which might be for the good of the Union, would render all the preceding and subsequent enumerations of power completely useless.

It would reduce the whole instrument to a single phrase, that of instituting a Congress with power to do whatever would be for the good of the United States; and, as they would be the sole judges of the good or evil, it would be also a power to do whatever evil they please....

2. The second general phrase is, "to make all laws *necessary* and proper for carrying into execution the enumerated powers." But they can all be carried into execution without a bank. A bank therefore is not *necessary*, and consequently not authorized by this phrase.

It has been urged that a bank will give great facility or convenience in the collection of taxes. Suppose this were true: yet the Constitution allows only the means which are *"necessary,"* not those which are merely *"convenient"* for effecting the enumerated powers. If such a latitude of construction be allowed to this phrase as to give any non-enumerated power, it will go to every one, for there is not one which ingenuity may not torture into a *convenience* in some instance *or other*, to *some one* of so long a list of enumerated powers. It would swallow up all the delegated powers, and reduce the whole to one power, as before observed. Therefore it was that the Constitution restrained them to the *necessary* means, that is to say, to those means without which the grant of power would be nugatory....

Source: Paul Leicester Ford, ed., *The Federalist: A Commentary on the Constitution of the United States by Alexander Hamilton, James Madison and John Jay edited with notes, illustrative documents and a copious index* (New York, 1898), 651–653.

Opinion on the Constitutionality of a National Bank
Alexander Hamilton

February 23, 1791

The Secretary of the Treasury having perused with attention the papers containing the opinions of the Secretary of State and Attorney-General, concerning the constitutionality of the bill for establishing a National Bank, proceeds, according to the order of the President, to submit the reasons which have induced him to entertain a different opinion....

...In entering upon the argument, it ought to be premised that the objections of the Secretary of State and Attorney General are founded on a general denial of the authority of the United States to erect corporations. The latter, indeed, expressly admits, that if there be anything in the bill which is not warranted by the Constitution, it is the clause of incorporation.

Now it appears to the Secretary of the Treasury, that this *general principle* is *inherent* in the very *definition* of Government and *essential* to every step of the progress to be made by that of the United States, namely: That every power vested in a government is in its nature *sovereign*, and includes, by *force* of the *term*, a right to employ all the *means* requisite and fairly applicable to the attainment of the *ends* of such power, and which are not precluded by restrictions and exceptions specified in the Constitution, or not immoral, or not contrary to the *essential ends* of political society....

The main proposition here laid down, in its true signification is not to be questioned. It is nothing more than a consequence of this republican maxim, that all government is a delegation of power; but how much is delegated in each case, is a question of fact, to be made out by fair reasoning and construction, upon the particular provisions of the Constitution, taking as guides the general principles and general ends of governments.

It is not denied that there are implied as well as *express* powers, and that the former are as effectually delegated as the latter. And for the sake of accuracy it shall be mentioned, that there is another class of powers, which may be properly denominated *resulting* powers. It will not be doubted, that if the United States should make a conquest of any of the territories of its neighbors, they would possess sovereign jurisdiction over the conquered territory: This would rather be a result from the whole mass of the powers of the government, and from the nature of political society, than a consequence of either of the powers specially enumerated....

Then it follows, that as a power of erecting a corporation may as well be *implied* as any other thing, it may as well be employed as an *instrument* or mean whatever. The only question must be, in this, as in every other case, whether the mean to be employed, or in this instance, the corporation to be erected, has a natural relation to any of the acknowledged objects or lawful ends of the government? Thus a corporation may not be erected by Congress for superintending the police of the city of Philadelphia, because they are not authorized to regulate the police of that city. But one may be erected in relation to the collection of the taxes, or to the trade with foreign countries, or to the trade between the States, or with the Indian Tribes; because it is the province of the federal government to regulate those objects, and because it is incident to a general *sovereign* or *legislative* power to regulate a thing, to employ all the means which relate to its regulation to the best and greatest advantage....

To this mode of reasoning, respecting the right of employing all the means requisite to the execution of the specified powers of the government, it is objected, that none but necessary and proper means are to be employed; and the Secretary of State maintains, that no means are to be considered as necessary but those without which the grant of the power would be nugatory. Nay, so far does he go in his restrictive interpretation of the word, as even to make the case of necessity which shall warrant the constitutional exercise of the power, to depend on casual and temporary circumstances; an idea which alone refutes the construction. The expediency of exercising a particular power, at a particular time, must, indeed, depend on circumstances; but the constitutional right of exercising it must be uniform and invariable, the same to-day, as to-morrow....

Such a construction would beget endless uncertainty and embarrassment. The cases must be palpable and extreme, in which it could be pronounced, with certainty, that a measure was absolutely necessary; or one, without which, the exercise of a given power would be nugatory. There are few measures of any government which would stand so severe a test. To insist upon it, would be to make the criterion of the exercise of any implied power, a *case of extreme necessity*; which is rather a rule to justify the overleaping of the bounds of constitutional authority, than to govern the ordinary exercise of it....

This restrictive interpretation of the word *necessary* is also contrary to this sound maxim of construction; namely, that the powers contained in a constitution of government, especially those which concern the general administration of the affairs of a country, its finances, trade, defense, etc., ought to be construed liberally, in advancement of the public good. This rule does not depend on the particular form of a government, or on the particular demarcation of the boundaries of its powers, but on the nature and objects of government itself. The means by which national exigencies are to be provided for; national inconveniences obviated; national prosperity promoted; are of such infinite variety, extent, and complexity, that there must of necessity be great latitude of discretion in the selection and application of those means. Hence, consequently, the necessity and propriety of exercising the authorities intrusted to a government on principles of liberal construction....

Source: Alexander Hamilton, *The Argument of the Secretary of the Treasury upon the Constitutionality of a National Bank* (Philadelphia, 1791), 3, 4, 6–11.

Chisholm v. Georgia (1793)

In one of its earliest decisions, the United States Supreme Court determined the reach of the federal courts as established by the new Constitution. The case began when a citizen of South Carolina sued the state of Georgia to recover a debt stemming from goods supplied by the citizen to Georgia during the Revolution-

ary War. The question before the Court was: Do the federal courts have jurisdiction in this case? Georgia contended that its state sovereignty prevented the federal courts from claiming jurisdiction. Georgia's steadfast belief in its own sovereignty even prevented the state from sending any representatives to argue its position before the Supreme Court. Four of the five justices, however, disagreed with Georgia and declared that the federal courts did have jurisdiction in such a case. The following excerpt from Chief Justice John Jay's opinion elucidates the Court's interpretation of its role in the early Republic. The decision was greeted with an outcry from political leaders concerned that the judicial branch of the federal government had encroached on state sovereignty.

MR. CHIEF JUSTICE JAY, delivered the opinion of the court,

The question we are now to decide has been accurately stated, viz. Is a State suable by individual citizens of another State? It is said, that Georgia refuses to appear and answer to the Plaintiff in this action, because she is a Sovereign State, and therefore not liable to such actions....

Sovereignty is the right to govern; a nation or State-sovereign is the person or persons in whom that resides....

The...object of enquiry now presents itself, viz. whether suability is compatible with State sovereignty. Suability, by whom? Not a subject, for in this country there are none; not an inferior, for all the citizens being as to civil rights perfectly equal, there is not, in that respect, one citizen inferior to another. It is agreed, that one free citizen may sue another; the obvious dictates of justice, and purposes of society demanding it. It is agreed, that one free citizen may sue any number on whom process can be conveniently executed; nay, in certain cases one citizen may sue forty thousand; for where a corporation is sued, all the members of it are actually sued, though not personally, sued....

There is at least one strong undeniable fact...and that is this, any one State in the Union may sue another State, in this Court, that is, all the people of one State may sue all the people of another State. It is plain then, that a State may be sued, and hence it plainly follows, that suability and State sovereignty are not incompatible. As one State may sue another State in this Court, it is plain that no degradation to a State is thought to accompany her appearance in this Court....

Let us now proceed to enquire whether Georgia has not, by being a party to the national compact, consented to be suable by individual citizens of another State....

Prior to the date of the Constitution, the people had not any national tribunal to which they could resort for justice; the distribution of justice was then confined to State judicatories, in whose institution and organization the people of the other States had no participation, and over whom they had not the least controul. There was then no general Court of appellate jurisdiction, by whom the errors of State Courts, affecting either the nation at large or the citizens of any other State, could be revised and corrected. Each State was obliged to acquiesce in the measure of justice which another State might yield to her, or to her citizens; and that even in cases where State considerations were not always favorable to the most exact measure. There was danger that from this source animosities would in time result; and as the transition from animosities to hostilities was frequent in the history of independent States, a common tribunal for the termination of controversies became desirable, from motives both of justice and of policy....

Let us now turn to the Constitution....

If we attend to the words, we find them to be express, positive, free from ambiguity, and without room for such implied expressions: "The judicial power of the United States shall extend to controversies between a State and citizens of another State."

...The extension of the judiciary power of the United States to such controversies, appears to me to be wise, because it is honest, and because it is useful. It is honest, because it provides for doing justice without respect for persons, and by securing individual citizens as well as States, in their respective rights, performs the promise which every free Government makes to every free citizen, of equal justice and protection. It is useful, because it is honest, because it leaves not even the most obscure and friendless citizen without means of obtaining justice from a neighbouring State; because it obviates occasions of quarrels between States on account of the claims of their respective citizens; because it recognizes and strongly rests on this great moral truth, that justice is the same whether due from one man or a million, or from a million to one man; because it teaches and greatly appreciates the value of our free republican national Government, which places all our citizens on an equal footing, and enables each and every of them to obtain justice without any danger of being overborne by the weight and number of their opponents; and, because it brings into action, and enforces this great and glorious principle, that the people are the sovereign of this country, and consequently that fellow citizens and joint sovereigns cannot be degraded by appearing with each other in their own Courts to have their controversies determined. The people have reason to prize and rejoice in such valuable privileges; and they ought not to forget, that nothing but the free course of Constitutional law and Government can ensure the continuance and enjoyment of them.

For the reasons before given, I am clearly of opinion, that a State is suable by citizens of another State; but lest I should be understood in a latitude beyond my meaning, I think it necessary to subjoin this caution, viz, That such suability may nevertheless not extend to all the demands, and to every kind of action; there may be exceptions. For instance, I am far from being prepared to say that an individual may sue a State on bills of credit issued before the Constitution was established, and which were issued and received on the faith of the State, and at a time when no ideas or expectations of judicial interposition were entertained or contemplated.

Source: 2 Dallas 419 (1793).

Eleventh Amendment (1798)

John Jay could not make his decision stick. Congress swiftly drafted a Constitutional Amendment reversing Chisholm v. Georgia. *By 1798 enough states had ratified the proposed amendment to make it a part of the Constitution. Jay quit the Court in disgust.*

The judicial power of the United States shall not be construed to extend to any suit in law or equity, commenced or prosecuted against one of the United States by citizens of another state or by citizens or subjects of any foreign state.

Source: Francis Newton Thorpe, ed., *The Federal and State Constitutions, Colonial Charters, and other Organic Laws* (Washington, 1909), 1:30.

Congressional Debate on the Sedition Act & the Sedition Act (1798)

With the bitter rivalry between the Federalists and Republicans in full swing, the year 1796 marked the first time Americans put the constitutional system devised for electing the president of the United States into action. John Adams, a Federalist candidate, barely won in the Electoral College and under the system's original design, the vice presidency went to Republican Thomas Jefferson as the candidate who garnered the second-highest number of electoral votes. The campaign had been exceedingly bitter, and even though they were now yoked together in the executive branch, Federalists and Republicans continued to distrust each other. Federalists in Congress introduced a bill making it a crime to "write, print, utter, or publish" any "false, scandalous, and malicious writings against the government of the United States." Realizing the law could be used against them in the next presidential campaign, the Republicans cried foul. The debate that ensued in Congress highlights the problem of protecting civil liberties in a free society while simultaneously protecting the safety and security of the nation. Despite strong objections, Congress passed the law that came to be known as the "Sedition Act" of 1798.

Congressional Debate, June 16, 1798

MR. OTIS said, that the objections made against this bill are not such as he had anticipated. He expected to have heard the most elaborate harangues in favor of the liberty of the press, and on the right which ought to be allowed to censure men and measures, and such popular topics; but he did not foresee any objection arising from the Constitution.

He did not think it required much time or ability, however, to answer the objections produced on this occasion by the gentleman from Pennsylvania. If Congress have not the power of restraining seditious persons, it is extremely clear they have not the power which the Constitution says they have, of providing for the common defence and general welfare of the Union....

He thought the whole question resolved itself into this inquiry: has Congress the power to provide for the common defence and welfare of the country? And, if so, do we deem it essential to this end, that the proposed power should be given to the President, or to some other Department of Government? He thought it was; and if there be anything in the letter of the Constitution which would appear to bear a different construction, which he denied, it ought to be reconciled to other clauses and powers which impose the sacred and superior duty of providing for the safety of the country, and without which all our efforts against our enemy will prove vain and futile. In this case there was not a shadow of difficulty. Aliens may come hither under the laws of the States, and when they become dangerous they be may expelled by the laws of the Union...

MR. R. WILLIAMS said that, although there might, in his opinion be many objections against the passing of a bill of this kind, and though he believed it would be consistent with the rules of the House to show that impolicy, to induce the committee to strike out the first section, he should confine himself to the Constitutional question.

If the principle which the gentlemen from Massachusetts have drawn from the preamble of the Constitution, of providing for the common defence and welfare of the Union, be correct; it appeared to him unnecessary to have any other provision in the Constitution besides the preamble, as it may be inferred from that, that Congress has all power whatever. If such a construction be allowed, what becomes of the powers of the State Governments? This preamble of the Constitution would swallow up the whole.

Mr. W. conceived gentlemen erred in the very commencement of their arguments, in not considering how the General Government had grown out of the State Governments and from the people; for it is clear, if they had thus considered the matter, they must have seen that this Government can have no other power than what is given to it from the State Governments and by the people, in the Constitution.

Mr. W. would agree that, if the General Government were to be considered as possessing all power, and the State Governments and people as possessing none, then the arguments of gentlemen would apply; but, he believed, this was a ground that no gentleman could maintain....

Source: *The Debates and Proceedings of the Congress of the United States*, Fifth Congress, part 2 (Washington, 1851), 1959–1962

The "Sedition Act"

An Act in addition to the act, entitled "An act for the punishment of certain crimes against the United States."

SECT. 1. *Be it enacted by the Senate and House of Representatives of the United States of America, in Congress assembled,* That if any persons shall unlawfully combine or conspire together, with intent to oppose any measure or measures of the government of the United States, which are or shall be directed by proper authority, or to impede the operation of any law of the United States, or to intimidate or prevent any person holding a place or office in or under the government of the United States, from undertaking, performing or executing his trust or duty; and if any person or persons, with intent as aforesaid, shall counsel, advise or attempt to procure any insurrection, riot, unlawful assembly, or combination, whether such conspiracy, threatening, counsel, advice, or attempt shall have the proposed effect or not, he or they shall be deemed guilty of a high misdemeanor, and on conviction, before any court of the United States having jurisdiction thereof, shall be punished by a fine not exceeding five thousand dollars, and by imprisonment during a term not less than six months nor exceeding five years; and further, at the discretion of the court may be holden to find sureties for his good behaviour in such sum, and for such time, as the said court may direct.

SECT. 2. *And be it further enacted,* That if any person shall write, print, utter or publish, or shall cause or procure to be written, printed, uttered or published, or shall knowingly and willingly assist or aid in writing, printing, uttering or publishing any false, scandalous and malicious writing or writings against the government of the United States, or either house of the Congress of the United States, or the President of the United States, with intent to defame the said government, or either house of the said Congress, or the said President, or to bring them, or either of them, into contempt or disrepute; or to excite against them, or either or any of them, the hatred of the good people of the United States, or to stir up sedition within the United States, or to excite any unlawful combinations therein, for opposing or resisting any law of the United States, or any act of the President of the United States, done in pursuance of any such law, or of the powers in him vested by the constitution of the United States, or to resist, oppose, or defeat any such law or act or to aid, encourage or abet any hostile designs of any foreign nation against the United States, their people or government, then such person, being thereof convicted before any court of the United States having jurisdiction thereof, shall be punished by a fine not exceeding two thousand dollars, and by imprisonment not exceeding two years.

SECT. 3. *And be it further enacted and declared,* That if any person shall be prosecuted under this act, for the writing or publishing any libel aforesaid, it shall be lawful for the defendant, upon the trial of the cause, to give in evidence in his defence, the truth of the matter contained in the publication charged as a libel. And the jury who shall try the cause, shall have a right to determine the law and the fact, under the direction of the court, as in other cases.

SECT. 4. *And be it further enacted,* That this act shall continue and be in force until the third day of March, one thousand eight hundred and one, and no longer: Provided, that the expiration of the act shall not prevent or defeat a prosecution and punishment of any offence against the law, during the time it shall be in force.

Approved, July 14, 1798.

Source: Richard Peters, ed., The Public Statutes at Large of the United States of America (Boston, 1845), 1:596–597.

Virginia and Kentucky Resolutions (1798–1799)

Just as Republicans had feared, Federalists used the Sedition Act as a weapon to silence their political enemies. Republicans, however, controlled state legislatures in the south, and Virginia and Kentucky considered seceding from the Union. Thomas Jefferson advised against that, predicting that soon the "reign of witches" would soon pass. The two states did pass resolutions that fell just short of secession. Authored by Thomas Jefferson and James Madison, the Virginia and Kentucky Resolutions clearly articulated positions on state sovereignty and state rights. Jefferson wrote the Kentucky resolutions, guided through the legislature by John Breckenridge, declaring the Alien and Sedition Acts unconstitutional. Madison wrote the Virginia Resolutions.

By the time he came to write the Virginia Resolutions, Madison no longer believed important points he had advanced in the Federalist Papers. In Federalist No. 10, he had confidently predicted that in a large republic no faction would be able to take power and oppress minority rights. By 1798, Madison had lived to see a faction — for that is how he saw the Federalists — do exactly what he had once thought impossible. In response he reconfigured his conception of the Constitution, now seeing it as a compact of the states. Madison, in fact, went further than Jefferson. Unlike the Kentucky Resolutions, the Virginia Resolutions said the states had the power to "interpose" their authority between their citizens and unconstitutional acts of Congress.

These resolutions did not nullify the Alien and Sedition Acts. All Jefferson and Madison did, really, was ask other states to agree with their criticism of the laws and their view of the Constitution. Other states did no such thing. Nonetheless, these resolutions proved powerfully influential. Reprinted for decades, they remained in print in 1861, when the South seceded from the Union. Southern secessionists cited these documents as justification for their actions. This version comes from an 1850 edition published in Richmond, Virginia.

Virginia Resolutions in the House of Delegates

Dec'r. 21st, 1798

Resolved, That the General Assembly of Virginia doth un-equivocally express a firm resolution to maintain and defend the Constitution of the United States, and the Constitution of this state, against every aggression, either foreign or domestic, and that it will support the government of the United States in all measures warranted by the former.

That this Assembly most solemnly declares a warm attachment to the union of the States, to maintain which, it pledges all its powers; and that for this end, it is its duty, to watch over and oppose every infraction of those principles, which constitute the only basis of that union, because a faithful observance of them can alone secure its existence, and the public happiness.

That this Assembly doth explicitly and peremptorily declare, that it views the powers of the Federal Government as resulting from the compact, to which the States are parties, as limited by the plain sense and intention of the instrument constituting that compact; as no farther valid than they are authorised by the grants enumerated in the compact; and that in case of a deliberate, palpable, and dangerous exercise of other powers not granted by the said compact, the States, who are parties thereto, have the right, and are in duty bound, to interpose for arresting the progress of the evil, and for maintaining within their respective limits, the authorities, rights and liberties appertaining to them.

That the General Assembly doth also express its deep regret that a spirit has in sundry instances been manifested by the Federal Government, to enlarge its powers by forced constructions of the constitutional charter which defines them; and that indications have appeared of a design to expound certain general phrases (which having been copied from the very limited grant of powers in the former articles of confederation, were the less liable to be misconstrued), so as to destroy the meaning and effect of the particular enumeration, which necessarily explains and limits the general phrases, and so as to consolidate the States by degrees into one sovereignty, the obvious tendency and inevitable result of which would be, to transform the present republican system of the United States, into an absolute, or at best, a mixed monarchy.

That the General Assembly doth particularly protest against the palpable and alarming infractions of the Constitution, in the two late cases of the "alien and sedition acts," passed at the last session of Congress, the first of which exercises a power nowhere delegated to the Federal Government; and which by uniting legislative and judicial powers, to those of executive, subverts the general principles of free government, as well as the particular organization and positive provisions of the federal Constitution; and the other of which acts exercises in like manner a power not delegated by the Constitution, but on the contrary expressly and positively forbidden by one of the amendments thereto; a power which more than any other ought to produce universal alarm, because it is leveled against that right of freely examining public characters and measures, and of free communication among the people thereon, which has ever been justly deemed, the only effectual guardian of every other right.

That this State having by its convention which ratified the federal Constitution, expressly declared, "that among other essential rights, the liberty of conscience and of the press cannot be cancelled, abridged, restrained, or modified by any authority of the United States," and from its extreme anxiety to guard these rights from every possible attack of sophistry or ambition, having with other States recommended an amendment for that purpose, which amendment was in due time annexed to the Constitution, it would mark a reproachful inconsistency and criminal degeneracy, if an indifference were now shown to the most palpable violation of one of the rights thus declared and secured, and to the establishment of a precedent which may be fatal to the other.

That the good people of this commonwealth having ever felt and continuing to feel the most sincere affection for their brethren of the other States, the truest anxiety for establishing and perpetuating the union of all, and the most scrupulous fidelity to that Constitution which is the pledge of mutual friendship, and the instrument of mutual happiness, the General Assembly doth solemnly appeal to the like dispositions of the other States, in confidence that they will concur with this commonwealth in declaring, as it does hereby declare, that the acts aforesaid are unconstitutional, and that the necessary and proper measures will be taken by each, for co-operating with this State in maintaining unimpaired the authorities, rights, and liberties, reserved to the States respectively, or to the people.

That the Governor be desired to transmit a copy of the foregoing resolutions to the executive authority of each of the other States, with a request, that the same may be communicated to the Legislature thereof. And that a copy be furnished to each of the senators and representatives, representing this State in the Congress of the United States.

Source: *The Virginia Report of 1799–1800, Touching the Alien and Sedition Laws; Together with the Virginia Resolutions* (Richmond, 1850), 22–23.

Kentucky Resolutions

Nov. 17, 1798

Resolved, That the several states composing the United States of America, are not united on the principle of unlimited submission to their general government; but that by a compact, under the style and title of a Constitution for the United States, and of amendments thereto, they constituted a general government for special purposes, delegated to that government certain definite powers, reserving, each state to itself, the residuary mass of right to their own self-government; and that whensoever the general government assumes undelegated powers, its acts are unauthoritative, void, and of no force: That to this compact each state acceded as a state, and is an integral party, its co-states forming, as to itself, the other party: That the government created by this compact was not made the exclusive or final *judge* of the extent of the powers delegated to itself; since that would have made its discretion, and not the Constitution, the measure of its powers; but that, as in all other cases of compact among powers having no common judge, each party has an equal right to judge for itself, as well of infractions as of the mode and measure of redress....

Resolved, That it is true as a general principle, and is also expressly declared by one of the Amendments to the Constitution, that "the powers not delegated to the United States by the Constitution, nor prohibited by it to the states, are reserved to the states respectively, or to the people;" and that no power over the freedom of religion, freedom of speech, or freedom of the press, being delegated to the United States by the Constitution, nor prohibited by it to the states, all lawful powers respecting the same did of right remain, and were reserved to the states, or to the people; that thus was manifested their determination to retain to themselves the right of judging how far the licentiousness of speech and of the press may be abridged without lessening their useful freedom, and how far those abuses which cannot be separated from their use should be tolerated, rather than the use be destroyed; and thus also they guarded against all abridgment by the United States of the freedom of religious opinions and exercises, and retained to themselves the right of protecting the same, as this state, by a law passed on the general demand of its citizens, had already protected them from all human restraint or interference: and that in addition to this general principle and express declaration, another and more special provision has been made by one of the amendments to the Constitution, which expressly declares, that "Congress shall make no law respecting an establishment of religion, or prohibiting the free exercise thereof, or abridging the freedom of speech, or of the press," thereby guarding in the same sentence, and under the same words, the freedom of religion, of speech, and of the press, insomuch, that whatever violates either, throws down the sanctuary which covers the others, and that libels, falsehood, and defamation, equally with heresy and false religion, are withheld from the cognizance of federal tribunals: that therefore, the act of Congress of the United States, passed on the 14th day of July, 1798, entitled "An Act in addition to the act entitled An Act for the punishment of certain crimes against the United States," which does abridge the freedom of the press, is not law, but is altogether void, and of no force....

Resolved, That the construction applied by the General Government (as is evinced by sundry of their proceedings,) to those parts of the Constitution of the United States which delegate to Congress a power "to lay and collect taxes, duties, imposts, and excises; to pay the debts, and provide for the common defence and general welfare of the United States, and to make all laws which shall be necessary and proper for carrying into execution the powers vested by the Constitution in the Government of the United States, or in any department or officer thereof, goes to the destruction of all limits prescribed to their power by the Constitution: that words meant by that instrument to be subsidiary only to the execution of limited powers, ought not to be so construed as themselves to give unlimited powers, nor a part to be so taken, as to destroy the whole residue of the instrument: that the proceedings of the General Government under colour of these articles, will be a fit and necessary subject of revisal and correction, at a time of greater tranquility, while those specified in the preceding resolutions call for immediate redress.

Resolved, That the preceding resolutions be transmitted to the senators and representatives in Congress from this commonwealth, who are hereby enjoined to present the same to their respective house, and to use their best endeavors to procure, at the next session of Congress a repeal of the aforesaid and obnoxious acts,

Resolved, lastly, That the Governor of this commonwealth be, and is hereby authorized to communicate the preceding resolutions to the legislatures of the several states, to assure them that this commonwealth considers union for specified national purposes, and particularly to those specified in their late federal compact, to be friendly to the peace, happiness, and prosperity of all the states: that, faithful to that compact, according to the plain intent and meaning in which it was understood and acceded to by the several parties, it is sincerely anxious for its preservation: that it does also believe, that to take from the states all the powers of self-government, and transfer them to a general and consolidated government, without regard to the special delegations and reservations solemnly agreed to in that compact, is not for the peace, happiness or prosperity of these states: and that therefore, this commonwealth is determined, as it doubts not its co-states are, tamely to submit to undelegated, and consequently unlimited powers in no man or body of men on earth: that if the acts before specified should stand, these conclusions would flow from them; that the general government may place any act they think proper on the list of crimes, and punish it themselves, whether enumerated or not enumerated by the Constitution, as cognizable by them; that they may transfer its cognizance to the President or any other person, who may himself be the accuser, counsel, judge and jury, whose *suspicions* may be the evidence, his order the sentence, his officer the executioner, and his breast the sole record of the transaction; that a very numerous and valuable description of the inhabitants of these states being, by this precedent, reduced, as outlaws to the absolute dominion of one man, and the barrier of the Constitution thus swept away for us all, no rampart now remains against the passions and the powers of a majority in Congress, to protect from a like exportation or other more grievous punishment the minority of the same body, the legislatures, judges, governors, and counsellors of the states, nor their other peaceable inhabitants who may venture to reclaim the constitutional rights and liberties of the states and people, or who for other causes, good or bad, may be obnoxious to the views, or marked by the suspicions of the President, or be thought dangerous to his or their elections, or other interests, public or personal: that the friendless alien has indeed been selected as the safest subject of a first experiment; but the citizen will soon follow, or rather has already followed; for, already has a sedition-act marked him as its prey: that these and successive acts of the same character, unless arrested at the threshold, may tend to drive these states into revolution and blood, and will furnish new calumnies against republican government, and new pretexts for those who wish it to be believed, that man cannot be governed but by a rod of iron: that it would be a dangerous delusion, were a confidence in the men of our choice, to silence our fears for the safety of our rights:

that confidence is everywhere the parent of despotism; free government is founded in jealousy, and not in confidence; it is jealousy and not confidence which prescribes limited constitutions to bind down those whom we are obliged to trust with power: that our Constitution has accordingly fixed the limits to which and no further our confidence may go; and let the honest advocate of confidence read the alien and sedition-acts, and say if the Constitution has not been wise in fixing limits to the government it created, and whether we should be wise in destroying those limits? Let him say what the government is if it be not a tyranny, which the men of our choice have conferred on our President, and the President of our choice has assented to and accepted, over the friendly strangers, to whom the mild spirit of our country and its laws have pledged hospitality and protection: that the men of our choice have more respected the bare suspicions of the President, than the solid rights of innocence, the claims of justification, the sacred force of truth, and the forms and substance of law and justice. In questions of power, then, let no more be heard of confidence in man, but bind him down from mischief by the chains of the Constitution. That this commonwealth does, therefore, call on its co-states for an expression of their sentiments on the acts concerning aliens, and for the punishment of certain crimes herein before specified, plainly declaring whether these acts are or are not authorized by the Federal compact? And it doubts not that their sense will be so announced, as to prove their attachment unaltered to limited government, whether general or particular, and that the rights and liberties of their co-states will be exposed to no dangers by remaining embarked in a common bottom with their own: That they will concur with this commonwealth in considering the said acts as so palpably against the Constitution as to amount to an undisguised declaration, that that compact is not meant to be the measure of the powers of the general government, but that it will proceed in the exercise over these states, of all powers whatsoever: That they will view this as seizing the rights of the states, and consolidating them in the hands of the general government with a power assumed to bind the states, (not merely in cases made federal,) but in all cases whatsoever, by laws made, not with their consent, but by others against their consent: That this would be to surrender the form of government we have chosen, and to live under one deriving its powers form its own will, and not from our authority ....

Source: The Virginia Report of 1799–1800 Touching the Alien and Sedition Laws; Together with the Virginia Resolutions (Richmond, 1850), 162–166.

6.

The Marshall Court

John Marshall is so closely identified with the Supreme Court's beginnings that it is easy to forget that he was not the first Chief Justice of the United States. By 1800, the Supreme Court had decided over one hundred cases. A critical sea change in the Court's evolution, however, came with President John Adams' appointment of John Marshall as chief justice. Marshall presided over the nation's high court from 1801 until his death in 1835, years that coincided with a period of tremendous growth and change for the young nation. In contrast to John Jay's unhappy experience, Marshall profoundly shaped both the Supreme Court and the nation at large, becoming one of the most highly esteemed justices in American history.

Marshall kept alive a vision of a strong national government after the Jeffersonian Republicans swept the Federalists from power in the election of 1800. A brilliant legal and political strategist, Marshall elevated the prestige of the Supreme Court to make it the co-equal of the executive and legislative branches. His forceful intelligence fashioned clear doctrine from the chaos of fact flowing into his Court. The effect was to add weight and meaning to the opinions, as the Court now spoke in a single, clear voice. He also adhered to the Federalist goal of developing the nation's commerce and industry. He established the rule of law in way that respected and guarded private property, making opportunities for entrepreneurs. Marshall envisioned a national market unimpeded by provincialism and neighborhood prejudice. Today, economic historians agree that the Marshall Court established a solid legal foundation that stabilized market capitalism's early, chaotic years and enabled the American economy to grow and thrive.

The Marshall Court also blocked a series of challenges to federal authority coming from the states. As a steadfast adherent of Alexander Hamilton's theory of "implied powers," Marshall's opinions clearly articulated the basis for a broad interpretation of federal power under the Constitution. In a number of ways, then, John Marshall's influence on the development of the nation outweighs most of the men who served as president during his long tenure on the Court.

Marbury v. Madison (1803)

In the landmark election of 1800, Thomas Jefferson and the Republicans swept the Federalists from national power. After Jefferson's election but before his party actually took power, the lame-duck Congress enacted the Organic Act for the District of Columbia, allowing the president to appoint justices of the peace. These low-ranking judges, the Federalists thought, would maintain order by jailing rioting Jeffersonians. In his last hours as president, John Adams appointed forty-two justices of the peace, all loyal Federalists, among them, William Marbury. Although signed by President Adams, a number of these commissions were never actually delivered to the intended recipients. Seeing an extraordinary chance to best his political rival John Marshall, President Thomas Jefferson forbade his Secretary of State, James Madison, to deliver the commissions. William Marbury, using section thirteen of the Judiciary Act of 1789 (see pages 134-135), went directly to the U.S. Supreme Court for help. Marbury asked the Court to take "original jurisdiction" rather than going through the appeal process. Marbury's lawyer, Charles Lee, asked the Court to issue an order (called a **writ of mandamus***) forcing Madison to hand over the commissions.*

Article III of the Constitution allows the Court original jurisdiction only in cases "affecting Ambassadors, other public Ministers and Consuls, and those in which a State shall be a Party." Since Marbury and Lee had gone directly to the Supreme Court in a case not covered by Article III, they asked the Court to do something not covered by the Constitution. Lee argued that Congress could grant original jurisdiction in cases not mentioned by the Constitution. Since Lee did not even pretend that Article III covered his case, his argument allowed — perhaps required — Marshall to expound on the powers of the Court and the Constitution. Marshall employed the established legal precedent of **judicial review** *to declare section thirteen unconstitutional because its provision allowing Marbury's case to originate in the Supreme Court conflicted with Article III of the Constitution. Thus, he simultaneously avoided a confrontation with the Executive and exercised the Court's power over Congress. Marshall's skillful maneuvering through this political thicket bolstered the Court's authority among the three branches of the federal government.*

MR. CHIEF JUSTICE MARSHALL delivered the opinion of the Court.

It is...decidedly the opinion of the court, that when a commission has been signed by the president, the appointment is made; and that the commission is complete, when the seal of the United States has been affixed to it by the secretary of state....

To withhold his commission, therefore, is an act deemed by the court not warranted by the law, but violative of a vested legal right....

It remains to be enquired whether....

[Marbury] is entitled to the remedy for which he applies....
The act to establish the judicial courts of the United States authorizes the Supreme Court to "issue writs of mandamus in cases warranted by the principles and usages of law, to any courts appointed, or persons holding office, under the authority of the United States."

The Secretary of State, being a person holding an office under the authority of the United States, is precisely within the letter of the description; and if this court is not authorized to issue a writ of mandamus to such an officer, it must be because the law is unconstitutional, and therefore incapable of conferring the authority, and assigning the duties which its words purport to confer and assign.

The constitution vests the whole judicial power of the United States in one Supreme Court, and such inferior courts as congress shall, from time to time, ordain and establish. This power is expressly extended to all cases arising under the laws of the United States; and, consequently, in some form, may be exercised over the present case; because the right claimed is given by a law of the United States.

In the distribution of this power it is declared that "the Supreme Court shall have original jurisdiction in all cases affecting ambassadors, other public ministers and consuls, and those in which a state shall be a party. In all other cases, the Supreme Court shall have appellate jurisdiction"....

It has been stated at the bar that the appellate jurisdiction may be exercised in a variety of forms, and that if it be the will of the legislature that a mandamus should be used for that purpose, that will must be obeyed. This is true, yet the jurisdiction must be appellate, not original.

It is the essential criterion of appellate jurisdiction, that it does not create that cause. Although, therefore, a mandamus may be directed to courts, yet to issue such a writ to an officer for the delivery of a paper, is in effect the same as to sustain an original jurisdiction. Neither is it necessary in such a case as this, to enable the court to exercise its appellate jurisdiction.

The authority, therefore, given to the Supreme Court, by the act establishing the judicial courts of the United States, to issue writs of mandamus to public officers, appears not to be warranted by the constitution....

It is not entirely unworthy of observation that in declaring what shall be the *supreme law of the land,* the *constitution* itself is first mentioned; and not the laws of the United States generally, but those only which shall be made in *pursuance* of the constitution, have that rank.

Thus, the particular phraseology of the constitution of the United States confirms and strengthens the principle, supposed to be essential to all written constitutions, that a law repugnant to the constitution is void; and that courts, as well as other departments, are bound by that instrument.

Source: 1 Cranch 137 (1803).

Fletcher v. Peck (1810)

This case arose from a scandal known as the Yazoo land fraud. In 1795, the state legislature of Georgia granted 35 million acres of land (roughly the size of Alabama and Mississippi today) to four land companies for the token price of one and a half cents per acre, although lawmakers voting for the sale had been bribed by the companies. Angry voters struck back at the polls, and in 1796 a new legislature repealed the grant, taking back the land as the voters had demanded. But before the rescinding took effect, the land companies had sold off the land to new buyers, including one Robert Fletcher of New Hampshire. Fletcher now found his title to 15,000 acres, which he had believed he purchased legally, in doubt. In 1803 Fletcher used the so-called diversity of citizenship clause of the Constitution (found in Article III, section 2) to bring his case into federal court. He chose to sue John Peck, who was involved in the land company but lived in Massachusetts. In fact, Fletcher and Peck were in collusion, both wanted the rescinding law declared unconstitutional. The case really stemmed from an effort by the New England Mississippi Land Company to build a stronger case for its title to the Yazoo lands. In addition to Peck, leading politicians owned stock in the com-

pany, and Alexander Hamilton (along with a speculator named Robert Goodloe Harper) devised the strategy of going to federal court. Organizing the case as a suit between individuals circumvented the Eleventh Amendment ban on private suits against states even though Georgia was clearly the real target of the litigation. In 1810, the U.S. Supreme Court agreed to hear the case. John Marshall framed his opinion to address both the issue of states' legal responsibility to uphold covenants into which they enter, and to reaffirm states' obligations to conduct their business within the boundaries established in the federal Constitution. Scholars agree that this case is one of Marshall's most important for its assertion of national power over localism and its protection of vested property rights.

MR. CHIEF JUSTICE MARSHALL delivered the opinion of the court.

...The lands in controversy vested absolutely in James Gunn and others, the original grantees, by the conveyance of the governor, made in pursuance of an act of assembly to which the legislature was fully competent. Being thus in full possession of the legal estate, they, for a valuable consideration, conveyed portions of the land to those who were willing to purchase. If the original transaction was infected with fraud, these purchasers did not participate in it, and had no notice of it. They were innocent. Yet the legislature of Georgia has involved them in the fate of the first parties to the transaction, and, if the act be valid, has annihilated their rights also....

In this case the legislature may have had ample proof that the original grant was obtained by practices which can never be too much reprobated, and which would have justified its abrogation so far as respected those to whom crime was imputable. But the grant, when issued, conveyed an estate in fee-simple to the grantee, clothed with all the solemnities which law can bestow. This estate was transferrable; and those who purchased parts of it were not stained by that guilt which infected the original transaction. Their case is not distinguishable from the ordinary case of purchasers of a legal estate without knowledge of any secret fraud which might have led to the emanation of the original grant. According to the well known course of equity, their rights could not be affected by such fraud. Their situation was the same, their title was the same, with that of every other member of the community who holds land by regular conveyances from the original patentee.

Is the power of the legislature competent to the annihilation of such title, and to a resumption of the property thus held?

The principle asserted is, that one legislature is competent to repeal any act which a former legislature was competent to pass; and that one legislature cannot abridge the powers of a succeeding legislature.

The correctness of this principle, so far as respects general legislation, can never be controverted. But, if an act be done under a law, a succeeding legislature cannot undo it. The past cannot be recalled by the most absolute power. Conveyances have been made, those conveyances have vested legal estates, and, if those estates may be seized by the sovereign authority, still, that they originally vested is a fact, and cannot cease to be a fact.

When, then, a law is in its nature a contract, when absolute rights have vested under that contract, a repeal of the law cannot devest those rights; and the act of annulling them, if legitimate, is rendered so by a power applicable to the case of every individual in the community....

The validity of this rescinding act, then, might well be doubted, were Georgia a single sovereign power. But Georgia cannot be viewed as a single, unconnected, sovereign power, on whose legislature no other restrictions are imposed than may be found in its own constitution. She is a part of a large empire; she is a member of the American union; and that union has a constitution the supremacy of which all acknowledge, and which imposes limits to the legislatures of the several states, which none claim a right to pass. The constitution of the United States declares that no state shall pass any bill of attainder, ex post facto law, or law impairing the obligation of contracts.

Does the case now under consideration come within this prohibitory section of the constitution?

In considering this very interesting question, we immediately ask ourselves what is a contract? Is a grant a contract?

A contract is a compact between two or more parties, and is either executory or executed. An executory contract is one in which a party binds himself to do, or not to do, a particular thing; such was the law under which the conveyance was made by the governor. A contract executed is one in which the object of contract is performed; and this, says Blackstone, differs in nothing from a grant. The contract between Georgia and the purchasers was executed by the grant. A contract executed, as well as one which is executory, contains obligations binding on the parties. A grant, in its own nature, amounts to an extinguishment of the right of the grantor, and implies a contract not to reassert that right. A party is, therefore, always estopped by his own grant.

Since, then, in fact, a grant is a contract executed, the obligation of which still continues, and since the constitution uses the general term contract, without distinguishing between those which are executory and those which are executed, it must be construed to comprehend the latter as well as the former. A law annulling conveyances between individuals, and declaring that the grantors should stand seized of their former estates, notwithstanding those grants, would be as repugnant to the constitution as a law discharging the vendors of property from the obligation of executing their contracts by conveyances. It would be strange if a contract to convey was secured by the constitution, while an absolute conveyance remained unprotected....

It is, then, the unanimous opinion of the court, that, in this case, the estate having passed into the hands of a purchaser for a valuable consideration, without notice, the state of Georgia was restrained, either by general principles which are common to our free institutions, or by the particular provisions of the constitution of the United States, from passing a law whereby the estate of the plaintiff in the premises so purchased could be constitutionally and legally impaired and rendered null and void....

Source: 6 Cranch 87 (1810)

Dartmouth College v. Woodward (1819)

Dartmouth College was incorporated in 1769 via a royal charter granted by King George III. In 1816 the Jeffersonian-controlled state legislature of New Hampshire annulled the royal charter and put the college, where good Federalists liked to send their children to school, under state control, appointing a new board of trustees. Members of the old board, however, believed King George's charter constituted a valid contract and filed a lawsuit to continue their control of the college. As he did in Fletcher v. Peck, *Marshall enforced the Constitution's prohibition against any state violating the obligation of contracts. As in* Fletcher v. Peck, *Marshall defined "contract" very broadly. In his construction, even charters issued by the King of England must be enforced by the law. The long-term effect of Marshall's vigorous defense of contracts in this case proved to be profound for the nation's history. Coming at the dawn of America's industrial revolution, the decision helped to create a stable legal environment in which industrial capitalism could thrive. Investors could advance money to entrepreneurs confident that their contracts would be enforced in federal court. The number of business corporations multiplied after this decision; 50 existed in 1819; by 1830 New England alone had nearly 1,900. In a concurring opinion, Justice Joseph Story established the basis on which states would regulate corporations for the rest of the nineteenth century.*

MR. CHIEF JUSTICE MARSHALL delivered the opinion of the Court .

...The title of the plaintiffs originates in a charter dated the 13th day December, in the year 1769, incorporating twelve persons therein mentioned, by the name of "The Trustees of Dartmouth College," granting to them and their successors the usual corporate privileges and powers, and authorizing the trustees, who are to govern the college, to fill up all vacancies which may be created in their own body.

The defendant claims under three acts of the legislature of New-Hampshire, the most material of which was passed on the 27th of June, 1816, and is entitled, "an act to amend the charter, and enlarge and improve the corporation of Dartmouth College." Among other alterations in the charter, this act increases the number of trustees to twenty-one, gives the appointment of the additional members to the executive of the State, and creates a board of overseers, with power to inspect and control the most important acts of the trustees. This board consists of twenty-five persons. The president of the senate, the speaker of the house of representatives, of New-Hampshire, and the governor and lieutenant governor of Vermont, for the time being, are to be members ex officio. The board is to be completed by the governor and council of New-Hampshire, who are also empowered to fill all vacancies which may occur. The acts of the 18th and 26th of December are supplemental to that of the 27th of June, and are principally intended to carry that act into effect.

The majority of the trustees of the college have refused to accept this amended charter, and have brought this suit for the corporate property, which is in possession of a person holding by virtue of the acts which have been stated.

It can require no argument to prove, that the circumstances of this case constitute a contract. An application is made to the crown for a charter to incorporate a religious and literary institution. In the application, it is stated that large contributions have been made for the object, which will be conferred on the corporation, as soon as it shall be created. The charter is granted, and on its faith the property is conveyed. Surely in this transaction every ingredient of a complete and legitimate contract is to be found....

...[I]t has been argued, that the word "contract," in its broadest sense, would comprehend the political relations between the government and its citizens, would extend to offices held within a State for State purposes, and to many of those laws concerning civil institutions, which must change with circumstances, and be modified by ordinary legislation; which deeply concern the public, and which, to preserve good government, the public judgment must control. That even marriage is a contract, and its obligations are effected by the laws respecting divorces. That the clause in the constitution, if construed in its greatest latitude, would prohibit these laws. Taken in its broad unlimited sense, the clause would be an unprofitable and vexatious interference with the internal concerns of a State, would unnecessarily and unwisely embarrass its legislation, and render immutable those civil institutions, which are established for purposes of internal government, and which, to subserve those purposes, ought to vary with varying circumstances. That as the framers of the constitution could never have intended to insert in that instrument a provision so unnecessary, so mischievous, and so repugnant to its general spirit, the term "contract" must be understood as intended to guard against a power of at least doubtful utility, the abuse of which had been extensively felt; and to restrain the legislature in future from violating the right to property. That anterior to the formation of the constitution, a course of legislation had prevailed in many, if not in all, of the States, which weakened the confidence of man in man, and embarrassed all transactions between individuals, by dispensing with a faithful performance of engagements. To correct this mischief, by restraining the power which produced it, the State legislatures were forbidden "to pass any law impairing the obligation of contracts," that is, of contracts respecting property, under which some individual could claim a right to something beneficial to himself; and that since the clause in the constitution must in construction receive some limitation, it may be confined, and ought to be confined, to cases of this description; to cases within the mischief it was intended to remedy....

A corporation is an artificial being, invisible, intangible, and existing only in contemplation of law. Being the mere creature of law, it possesses only those properties which the charter of its creation confers upon it, either expressly, or as incidental to its very existence. These are such as are supposed best calculated to effect the object for which it was created. Among the most important are immortality, and, if the expression may be allowed, individuality; properties, by which a perpetual succession of many persons are considered as the same, and may act as a single individual. They enable a corporation to manage its own affairs, and to hold property without the perplexing intricacies, the hazardous and endless necessity, of perpetual conveyances for the purpose of transmitting it from hand to hand. It is chiefly for the purpose of clothing bodies of men, in succession, with these qualities and capacities, that corporations were invented, and are in use. By these means, a perpetual succession of individuals are capable of acting for the promotion of the particular object, like one immortal being. But this being does not share in the civil government of the country, unless that be the purpose for which it was created. Its immortality no more confers on it political power, or a political character, than immortality would confer such power or character on a natural person. It is no more a State instrument, than a natural person exercising the same powers would be.

If, then, a natural person, employed by individuals in the education of youth, or for the government of a seminary in which youth is educated, would not become a public officer, or be considered as a member of the civil government, how is it, that this artificial being, created by law, for the purpose of being employed by the same individuals for the same purposes, should become a part of the civil government of the country? Is it because its existence, its capacities, its powers, are given by law? Because the government has given it the power to take and to hold property in a particular form, and for particular purposes, has the government a consequent right substantially to change that form, or to vary the purposes to which the property is to be applied? This principle has never been asserted or recognized, and is supported by no authority. Can it derive aid from reason?...

The opinion of the Court, after mature deliberation, is, that this is a contract, the obligation of which cannot be impaired, without violating the constitution of the United States. This opinion appears to us to be equally supported by reason, and by the former decisions of this Court.

MR. JUSTICE STORY, concurring.

In my judgment it is perfectly clear, that any act of a legislature which takes away any powers or franchises vested by its charter in a private corporation or its corporate officers, or which restrains or controls the legitimate exercise of them, or transfers them to other persons, with its assent, is a violation of the obligations of the charter. If the legislature means to claim such an authority, it must be reserved in the grant. The charter of Dartmouth College contains no such reservation; and I am, therefore, bound to declare, that the acts of the legislature of New Hampshire, now in question, do impair the obligations of that charter, and are, consequently, null and void.

Source: 4 Wheaton 518 (1819).

McCulloch v. Maryland (1819)

The charter that created the Bank of the United States expired in 1811, and the Jeffersonians, who controlled the legislative and executive branches of the federal government, prevented the Bank from getting a new charter. Thus, when the United States plunged into the War of 1812, it did so without a central monetary authority. By 1816, the nation's developing industrial economy served to convince even many Jeffersonians of the institution's advantages, and Congress passed a new law incorporating a second Bank of the United States for the next twenty years. The second Bank of the United States stood at the center of Henry Clay's American system, which envisioned internal improvements paid for by U.S. taxpayers and a tariff to protect and promote U.S. manufacturing. But opponents feared that centralizing control of the nation's economy in a creature created by the federal legislature would take power away from the states.

The state of Maryland challenged the Bank by passing a state law that taxed its branch in Baltimore. Maryland only wanted the bank to pay $15,000, not enough to impede its operations. Nonetheless, the Bank's cashier, William McCulloch, refused to pay the tax, arguing that a state could not exercise such a power over an agency of the federal government. Lawyers for Maryland contended that Congress had no power to establish the Bank in the first place as the Constitution did not specifically empower the federal legislature to create corporations. Chief Justice Marshall, however, unequivocally upheld federal over state authority. Marshall's defense of the implied powers doctrine reaffirmed Alexander Hamilton's original argument for the Bank's constitutionality. His opinion stands today as one of the most articulate endorsements of the Supremacy Clause (Article VI) in American constitutional discourse.

MR. CHIEF JUSTICE MARSHALL delivered the opinion of the Court.

In the case now to be determined, the defendant, a sovereign State, denies the obligation of a law enacted by the legislature of the Union, and the plaintiff, on his part, contests the validity of an act which has been passed by the legislature of that State. The constitution of our country, in its most interesting and vital parts, is to be considered; the conflicting powers of the government of the Union and of its members, as marked in that constitution, are to be discussed; and an opinion given, which may essentially influence the great operations of the government. No tribunal can approach such a question without a deep sense of its importance, and of the awful responsibility involved in its decision. But it must be decided peacefully, or remain a source of hostile legislation, perhaps of hostility of a still more serious nature; and if it is to be so decided, by this tribunal alone can the decision be made. On the Supreme Court of the United States has the constitution of our country devolved this important duty.

The first question made in the cause is, has Congress power to incorporate a bank?...

In discussing this question, the counsel for the State of Maryland have deemed it of some importance, in the construction of the constitution, to consider that instrument not as emanating from the people, but as the act of sovereign and independent States. The powers of the general government, it has been said, are delegated by the States, who alone are truly sovereign; and must be exercised in subordination to the States, who alone possess supreme dominion.

It would be difficult to sustain this proposition....

The government proceeds directly from the people; is "ordained and established" in the name of the people; and is declared to be ordained, "in order to form a more perfect union, establish justice, ensure domestic tranquillity, and secure the blessings of liberty to themselves and to their posterity." The assent of the States, in their sovereign capacity, is implied in calling a Convention, and thus submitting that instrument to the people. But the people were at perfect liberty to accept or reject it; and their act was final. It required not the affirmance, and could not be negatived, by the State governments. The constitution, when thus adopted, was of complete obligation, and bound the State sovereignties....

The government of the United States, then, though limited in its powers, is supreme; and its laws, when made in pursuance of the constitution, form the supreme law of the land, "any thing in the constitution or laws of any State to the contrary notwithstanding."

Among the enumerated powers, we do not find that of establishing a bank or creating a corporation. But there is no phrase in the instrument which, like the articles of confederation, excludes incidental or implied powers; and which requires that every thing granted shall be expressly and minutely described. Even the 10th amendment, which was framed for the purpose of quieting the excessive jealousies which had been excited, omits the word "expressly," and declares only that the powers "not delegated to the United States, nor prohibited to the States, are reserved to the States or to the people;" thus leaving the question, whether the particular power which may become the subject of contest has been delegated to the one government, or prohibited to the other, to depend on a fair construction of the whole instrument. The men who drew and adopted this amendment had experienced the embarrassments resulting from the insertion of this word in the articles of confederation, and probably omitted it to avoid those embarrassments....

Although, among the enumerated powers of government, we do not find the word "bank" or "incorporation," we find the great powers to lay and collect taxes; to borrow money; to regulate commerce; to declare and conduct a war; and to raise and support armies and navies. The sword and the purse, all the external relations, and no inconsiderable portion of the industry of the nation, are entrusted to its government. It can never be pretended that these vast powers draw after them others of inferior importance, merely because they are inferior. Such an idea can never be advanced. But it may with great reason be contended, that a government, entrusted with such ample powers, on the due execution of which the happiness and prosperity of the nation so vitally depends, must also be entrusted with ample means for their execution.... Can we adopt that construction, (unless the words imperiously require it,) which would impute to the framers of that instrument, when granting these powers for the public good, the intention of impeding their exercise by withholding a choice of means? If, indeed, such be the mandate of the constitution, we have only to obey; but that instrument does not profess to enumerate the means by which the powers it confers may be executed; nor does it prohibit the creation of a corporation, if the existence of such a being be essential to the beneficial exercise of those powers. It is, then, the subject of fair inquiry, how far such means may be employed.

It is not denied, that the powers given to the government imply the ordinary means of execution. That, for example, of raising revenue, and applying it to national purposes, is admitted to imply the power of conveying money from place to place, as the exigencies of the nation may require, and of employing the usual means of conveyance. But it is denied that the government has its choice of means; or, that it may employ the most convenient means, if, to employ them, it be necessary to erect a corporation.

On what foundation does this argument rest? On this alone: The power of creating a corporation, is one appertaining to sovereignty, and is not expressly conferred on Congress. This is true. But all legislative powers appertain to sovereignty. The original power of giving the law on any subject whatever, is a sovereign power; and if the government of the Union is restrained from creating a corporation, as a means for performing its functions, on the single reason that the creation of a corporation is an act of sovereignty; if the sufficiency of this reason be acknowledged, there would be some difficulty in sustaining the authority of Congress to pass other laws for the accomplishment of the same objects....

But the constitution of the United States has not left the right of Congress to employ the necessary means, for the execution of the powers conferred on the government, to general reasoning. To its enumeration of powers is added that of making "all laws which shall be necessary and proper, for carrying into execution the foregoing powers, and all other powers vested by this constitution, in the government of the United States, or in any department thereof."

The counsel for the State of Maryland have urged various arguments, to prove that this clause, though in terms a grant of power, is not so in effect; but is really restrictive of the general right, which might otherwise be implied, of selecting means for executing the enumerated powers....

But the argument on which most reliance is placed, is drawn from the peculiar language of this clause. Congress is not empowered by it to make all laws, which may have relation to the powers conferred on the government, but such only as may be "necessary and proper" for carrying them into execution. The word "necessary," is considered as controlling the whole sentence, and as limiting the right to pass laws for the execution of the granted powers, to such as are indispensable, and without which the power would be nugatory. That it excludes the choice of means, and leaves to Congress, in each case, that only which is most direct and simple....

We admit, as all must admit, that the powers of the government are limited, and that its limits are not to be transcended. But we think the sound construction of the constitution must allow to the national legislature that discretion, with respect to the means by which the powers it confers are to be carried into execution, which will enable that body to perform the high duties assigned to it, in the manner most beneficial to the people. Let the end be legitimate, let it be within the scope of the constitution, and all means which are appropriate, which are plainly adapted to that end, which are not prohibited, but consist with the letter and spirit of the constitution, are constitutional....

It being the opinion of the Court, that the act incorporating the bank is constitutional; and that the power of establishing a branch in the State of Maryland might be properly exercised by the bank itself, we proceed to inquire...[w]hether the State of Maryland may, without violating the constitution, tax that branch?

That the power of taxation is one of vital importance; that it is retained by the States; that it is not abridged by the grant of a similar power to the government of the Union; that it is to be concurrently exercised by the two governments: are truths which have never been denied. But, such is the paramount character of the constitution, that its capacity to withdraw any subject from the action of even this power, is admitted. The States are expressly forbidden to lay any duties on imports or exports, except what may be absolutely necessary for executing their inspection laws. If the obligation of this prohibition must be conceded — if it may restrain a State from the exercise of its taxing power on imports and exports; the same paramount character would seem to restrain, as it certainly may restrain, a State from such other exercise of this power, as is in its nature incompatible with, and repugnant to, the constitutional laws of the Union. A law, absolutely repugnant to another, as entirely repeals that other as if express terms of repeal were used.

On this ground the counsel for the bank place its claim to be exempted from the power of a State to tax its operations. There is no express provision for the case, but the claim has been sustained on a principle which so entirely pervades the constitution, is so intermixed with the materials which compose it, so interwoven with its web, so blended with its texture, as to be incapable of being separated from it, without rending it into shreds.

This great principle is, that the constitution and the laws made in pursuance thereof are supreme; that they control the constitution and laws of the respective States, and cannot be controlled by them. From this, which may be almost termed an axiom, other propositions are deduced as corollaries, on the truth or error of which, and on their application to this case, the cause has been supposed to depend. These are, 1st. that a power to create implies a power to preserve. 2nd. That a power to destroy, if wielded by a different hand, is hostile to, and incompatible with these powers to create and to preserve. 3d. That where this repugnancy exists, that authority which is supreme must control, not yield to that over which it is supreme....

That the power of taxing it by the States may be exercised so as to destroy it, is too obvious to be denied. But taxation is said to be an absolute power, which acknowledges no other limits than those expressly prescribed in the constitution, and like sovereign power of every other description, is trusted to the discretion of those who use it. But the very terms of this argument admit that the sovereignty of the State, in the article of taxation itself, is subordinate to, and may be controlled by the constitution of the United States. How far it has been controlled by that instrument must be a question of construction. In making this construction, no principle not declared, can be admissable, which would defeat the legitimate operations of a supreme government. It is of the very essence of supremacy to remove all obstacles to its action within its own sphere, and so to modify every power vested in subordinate governments, as to exempt its own operations from their own influence. This effect need not be stated in terms. It is so involved in the declaration of supremacy, so necessarily implied in it, that the expression of it could not make it more certain. We must, therefore, keep it in view while construing the constitution....

The sovereignty of a State extends to every thing which exists by its own authority, or is introduced by its permission; but does it extend to those means which are employed by Congress to carry into execution powers conferred on that body by the people of the United States? We think it demonstrable that it does not. Those powers are not given by the people of a single State. They are given by the people of the United States, to a government whose laws, made in pursuance of the constitution, are declared to be supreme. Consequently, the people of a single State cannot confer a sovereignty which will extend over them....

We are unanimously of opinion, that the law passed by the legislature of Maryland, imposing a tax on the Bank of the United States, is unconstitutional and void.

Source: 4 Wheaton 316 (1819).

Gibbons v. Ogden (1824)

This important case originated as a dispute between rival steamboat operators. In 1811 Robert Fulton and Robert Livingston persuaded the New York legislature to grant them a monopoly over steamboat transportation in New York waters. The law said that any vessel violating the monopoly could be confiscated. Despite such stern strictures, the law proved difficult to enforce and Fulton and Livingston had no luck persuading neighboring states to recognize their rights.

Fulton and Livingston then gave Aaron Ogden exclusive rights to steam navi-
gation across the Hudson River between New York and New Jersey. Thomas
Gibbons operated his own steamboat in competition with Ogden, relying on the
license he had obtained to operate in federal waters under the Federal Coasting
Act of 1793. But the men's dispute over business was also a matter of state ver-
sus federal authority, and in 1824 the U.S. Supreme Court agreed to hear the
case.

The Constitution gives Congress the power "to regulate commerce...among
the several states" (Article I, section 8). But the meaning of this clause, which
went to the heart of federalism and states' rights, remained controversial and
uncertain for decades. Alexander Hamilton had insisted that "among the
states," language gave Congress over all commercial activity, while Thomas Jef-
ferson had claimed Congress only had power to regulate commerce between
states. In this landmark decision, John Marshall settled the argument squarely
in favor of federal authority over transportation by defining the meaning of the
commerce clause broadly enough to include not just buying and selling but also
the means by which commerce was transported. At the same time, Marshall lim-
ited federal power to interstate commerce, not business conducted solely within
a state. Marshall agreed with Jefferson on that point. In the long run, this would
not matter as little commerce today takes place entirely within any one state. In
the nineteenth century, though, the states would regulate commerce more than
the Congress. Marshall's decision made Congress's power over interstate com-
merce virtually unchecked. From this precedent grew the national government's
authority to establish national transportation systems and, eventually, its power
to regulate the transported goods themselves.

MR. CHIEF JUSTICE MARSHALL delivered the opinion of the
Court, and, after stating the case, proceeded as follows....

[R]eference has been made to the political situation of these
States anterior to [the United States'] formation. It has been said
that they were sovereign, were completely independent, and were
connected with each other only by a league. This is true. But,
when these allied sovereigns converted their league into a government, they converted their Congress of Ambassadors, deputed
to deliberate on their common concerns and to enact laws on the
most interesting subjects, the whole character in which the States
appear underwent a change, the extent of which must be deter-

mined by a fair consideration of the instrument by which that change was effected.

This instrument contains the enumeration of powers expressly granted by the people to their government. It has been said that these powers ought to be construed strictly. But why ought they to be so construed? Is there one sentence in the Constitution which gives countenance to this rule?...What do gentlemen mean by "strict construction"? If they contend only against that enlarged construction, which would extend words beyond their natural and obvious import, we might question the application of the term, but should not controvert the principle. If they contend for that narrow construction which, in support of some theory not to be found in the Constitution, would deny to the government those powers which the words of the grant, as usually understood, import, and which are consistent with the general views of the objects of the instrument; for that narrow construction which would cripple the government and render it unequal to the object for which it is declared to be instituted, and to which the powers given, as fairly understood, render it competent; then we cannot perceive the propriety of this strict construction, nor adopt it as the rule by which the Constitution is to be expounded. As men whose intentions require no concealment generally employ the words which most directly and aptly express the ideas they intend to convey, the enlightened patriots who framed our Constitution, and the people who adopted it, must...have intended what they have said....

The words are, "Congress shall have power to regulate commerce with foreign nations, and among the several States, and with the Indian tribes."

The subject to be regulated is commerce; and our constitution being, as was aptly said at the bar, one of enumeration, and not of definition, to ascertain the extent of the power, it becomes necessary to settle the meaning of the word. The counsel for the appellee would limit it to traffic, to buying and selling, or the interchange of commodities, and do not admit that it comprehends navigation. This would restrict a general term, applicable to many objects, to one of its significations. Commerce, undoubtedly, is traffic, but it is something more: it is intercourse. It describes the commercial intercourse between nations, and parts of nations, in all its branches, and is regulated by prescribing rules for carrying on that intercourse. The mind can scarcely conceive a system for regulating commerce between nations, which shall exclude all laws concerning navigation, which shall be silent on the admission of the vessels of the one nation into the ports of the other, and be confined to prescribing rules for the conduct of individuals, in the actual employment of buying and selling, or of barter.

The word used in the Constitution, then, comprehends, and has been always understood to comprehend, navigation within its meaning, and a power to regulate navigation is expressly granted as if that term had been added to the word "commerce."

To what commerce does this power extend? The Constitution informs us, to commerce "with foreign nations, and among the several States, and with the Indian tribes."

It has, we believe, been universally admitted that these words comprehend every species of commercial intercourse between the United States and foreign nations. No sort of trade can be carried on between this country and any other to which this power does not extend. It has been truly said that "commerce," as the word is used in the Constitution, is a unit every part of which is indicated by the term.

If this be the admitted meaning of the word in its application to foreign nations, it must carry the same meaning throughout the sentence, and remain a unit, unless there be some plain intelligible cause which alters it.

The subject to which the power is next applied is commerce "among the several States." The word "among" means intermingled with. A thing which is among others is intermingled with them. Commerce among the States cannot stop at the external boundary line of each State, but may be introduced into the interior.

It is not only intended to say that these words comprehend that commerce which is completely internal, which is carried on between man and man in a State, or between different parts of the same State, and which does not extend to or affect other States.

Such a power would be inconvenient, and is certainly unnecessary.

Comprehensive as the word "among" is, it may very properly be restricted to that commerce which concerns more States than one. The phrase is not one which would probably have been selected to indicate the completely interior traffic of a State, because it is not an apt phrase for that purpose, and the enumeration of the particular classes of commerce to which the power was be extended would not have been made had the intention been to extend the power to every description.... The genius and character of the whole government seem to be that if action is to be applied to all the external concerns of the nation, and to those internal concerns which affect the States generally, but not to those which are completely within a particular State, which do not affect other States, and with which it is not necessary to interfere for the purpose of executing some of the general powers of the government. The completely internal commerce of a State, then, may be considered as reserved for the State itself.

But, in regulating commerce with foreign nations, the power of Congress does not stop at the jurisdictional lines of the several states. It would be a very useless power if it could not pass those lines. The commerce of the United States with foreign nations is that of the whole United States. Every district has a right to participate in it. The deep streams which penetrate our country in every direction pass through the interior of almost every State in the Union, and furnish the means of exercising this right. If Congress has the power to regulate it, that power must be exercised whenever the subject exists. If it exists within the States, if a foreign voyage may commence or terminate at a port within a State, then the power of Congress may be exercised within a State....

We are now arrived at the inquiry — What is this power?

It is the power to regulate; that is, to prescribe the rule by which commerce is to be governed. This power, like all others vested in Congress, is complete in itself, may be exercised to its utmost extent, and acknowledges no limitations, other than are prescribed in the constitution. These are expressed in plain terms, and do not affect the questions which arise in this case, or which have been discussed at the bar. If, as has always been understood, the sovereignty of Congress, though limited to specified objects, is plenary as to those objects, the power over commerce with foreign nations, and among the several States, is vested in Congress as absolutely as it would be in a single government, having in its constitution the same restrictions on the exercise of the power as are found in the constitution of the United States. The wisdom and the discretion of Congress, their identity with the people, and the influence which their constituents possess at elections, are, in this, as in many other instances, as that, for example, of declaring war, the sole restraints on which they have relied, to secure them from its abuse. They are the restraints on which the people must often rely solely, in all representative governments....

It has been contended that, if a law passed by a State, in the exercise of its acknowledged sovereignty, comes into conflict with a law passed by Congress in pursuance of the constitution, they affect the subject and each other like equal opposing powers.

But the framers of our constitution foresaw this state of things, and provided for it by declaring the supremacy not only of itself, but of the laws made in pursuance of it. The nullity of any act inconsistent with the constitution is produced by the declaration that the constitution is the supreme law. The appropriate application of that part of the clause which confers the same supremacy on laws and treaties is to such acts of the State Legislatures as do not transcend their powers, but, though enacted in the execution of acknowledged State powers, interfere with, or are contrary to, the laws of Congress made in pursuance of the constitution or some treaty under the authority of the United States. In every such case, the act of Congress or the treaty is supreme, and the law of the State, though enacted in the exercise of powers not converted, must yield to it....

Source: 9 Wheaton 1 (1824).

APPENDIX

Constitution of the United States

Preamble

We the people of the United States, in order to form a more perfect union, establish justice, insure domestic tranquility, provide for the common defense, promote the general welfare, and secure the blessings of liberty to ourselves and our posterity, do ordain and establish this Constitution for the United States of America.

Article I

Section 1. All legislative powers herein granted shall be vested in a Congress of the United States, which shall consist of a Senate and House of Representatives.

Section 2. The House of Representatives shall be composed of members chosen every second year by the people of the several states, and the electors in each state shall have the qualifications requisite for electors of the most numerous branch of the state legislature.

No person shall be a Representative who shall not have attained to the age of twenty five years, and been seven years a citizen of the United States, and who shall not, when elected, be an inhabitant of that state in which he shall be chosen.

Representatives and direct taxes shall be apportioned among the several states which may be included within this union, according to their respective numbers, which shall be determined by adding to the whole number of free persons, including those bound to service for a term of years, and excluding Indians not taxed, three fifths of all other Persons. The actual Enumeration shall be made within three years after the first meeting of the Congress of the

United States, and within every subsequent term of ten years, in such manner as they shall by law direct. The number of Representatives shall not exceed one for every thirty thousand, but each state shall have at least one Representative; and until such enumeration shall be made, the state of New Hampshire shall be entitled to chuse three, Massachusetts eight, Rhode Island and Providence Plantations one, Connecticut five, New York six, New Jersey four, Pennsylvania eight, Delaware one, Maryland six, Virginia ten, North Carolina five, South Carolina five, and Georgia three.

When vacancies happen in the Representation from any state, the executive authority thereof shall issue writs of election to fill such vacancies.

The House of Representatives shall choose their speaker and other officers; and shall have the sole power of impeachment.

Section 3. The Senate of the United States shall be composed of two Senators from each state, chosen by the legislature thereof, for six years; and each Senator shall have one vote.

Immediately after they shall be assembled in consequence of the first election, they shall be divided as equally as may be into three classes. The seats of the Senators of the first class shall be vacated at the expiration of the second year, of the second class at the expiration of the fourth year, and the third class at the expiration of the sixth year, so that one third may be chosen every second year; and if vacancies happen by resignation, or otherwise, during the recess of the legislature of any state, the executive thereof may make temporary appointments until the next meeting of the legislature, which shall then fill such vacancies.

No person shall be a Senator who shall not have attained to the age of thirty years, and been nine years a citizen of the United States and who shall not, when elected, be an inhabitant of that state for which he shall be chosen.

The Vice President of the United States shall be President of the Senate, but shall have no vote, unless they be equally divided.

The Senate shall choose their other officers, and also a President pro tempore, in the absence of the Vice President, or when he shall exercise the office of President of the United States.

The Senate shall have the sole power to try all impeachments. When sitting for that purpose, they shall be on oath or affirmation. When the President of the United States is tried, the Chief Justice shall preside: And no person shall be convicted without the concurrence of two thirds of the members present.

Judgment in cases of impeachment shall not extend further than to removal from office, and disqualification to hold and enjoy any office of honor, trust or profit under the United States: but the party convicted shall nevertheless be liable and subject to indictment, trial, judgment and punishment, according to law.

Section 4. The times, places and manner of holding elections for Senators and Representatives, shall be prescribed in each state by the legislature thereof; but the Congress may at any time by law make or alter such regulations, except as to the places of choosing Senators.

The Congress shall assemble at least once in every year, and such meeting shall be on the first Monday in December, unless they shall by law appoint a different day.

Section 5. Each House shall be the judge of the elections, returns and qualifications of its own members, and a majority of each shall constitute a quorum to do business; but a smaller number may adjourn from day to day, and may be authorized to compel the attendance of absent members, in such manner, and under such penalties as each House may provide.

Each House may determine the rules of its proceedings, punish its members for disorderly behavior, and, with the concurrence of two thirds, expel a member.

Each House shall keep a journal of its proceedings, and from time to time publish the same, excepting such parts as may in their judgment require secrecy; and the yeas and nays of the members of either House on any question shall, at the desire of one fifth of those present, be entered on the journal.

Neither House, during the session of Congress, shall, without the consent of the other, adjourn for more than three days, nor to any other place than that in which the two Houses shall be sitting.

Section 6. The Senators and Representatives shall receive a compensation for their services, to be ascertained by law, and paid out of the treasury of the United States. They shall in all cases, except treason, felony and breach of the peace, be privileged from arrest during their attendance at the session of their respective Houses, and in going to and returning from the same; and for any speech or debate in either House, they shall not be questioned in any other place.

No Senator or Representative shall, during the time for which he was elected, be appointed to any civil office under the authority of the United States, which shall have been created, or the emoluments whereof shall have been increased during such time: and no person holding any office under the United States, shall be a member of either House during his continuance in office.

Section 7. All bills for raising revenue shall originate in the House of Representatives; but the Senate may propose or concur with amendments as on other Bills.

Every bill which shall have passed the House of Representatives and the Senate, shall, before it become a law, be presented to the President of the United States; if he approve he shall sign it, but if not he shall return it, with his objections to that House in which it shall have originated, who shall enter the objections at large on their journal, and proceed to reconsider it. If after such reconsideration two thirds of that House shall agree to pass the bill, it shall be sent, together with the objections, to the other House, by which it shall likewise be reconsidered, and if approved by two thirds of that House, it shall become a law. But in all such cases the votes of both Houses shall be determined by yeas and nays, and the names of the persons voting for and against the bill shall be entered on the journal of each House respectively. If any bill shall not be returned by the President within ten days (Sundays excepted) after it shall have been presented to him, the same shall be a law, in like manner as if he had signed it, unless the Congress by their adjournment prevent its return, in which case it shall not be a law.

Every order, resolution, or vote to which the concurrence of the Senate and House of Representatives may be necessary (except on a question of adjournment) shall be presented to the President of the United States; and before the same shall take effect, shall be approved by him, or being disapproved by him, shall be repassed by two thirds of the Senate and House of Representatives, according to the rules and limitations prescribed in the case of a bill.

Section 8. The Congress shall have power to lay and collect taxes, duties, imposts and excises, to pay the debts and provide for the common defense and general welfare of the United States; but all duties, imposts and excises shall be uniform throughout the United States;

To borrow money on the credit of the United States;

To regulate commerce with foreign nations, and among the several states, and with the Indian tribes;

To establish a uniform rule of naturalization, and uniform laws on the subject of bankruptcies throughout the United States;

To coin money, regulate the value thereof, and of foreign coin, and fix the standard of weights and measures;

To provide for the punishment of counterfeiting the securities and current coin of the United States;

To establish post offices and post roads;

To promote the progress of science and useful arts, by securing for limited times to authors and inventors the exclusive right to their respective writings and discoveries;

To constitute tribunals inferior to the Supreme Court;

To define and punish piracies and felonies committed on the high seas, and offenses against the law of nations;

To declare war, grant letters of marque and reprisal, and make rules concerning captures on land and water;

To raise and support armies, but no appropriation of money to that use shall be for a longer term than two years;

To provide and maintain a navy;

To make rules for the government and regulation of the land and naval forces;

To provide for calling forth the militia to execute the laws of the union, suppress insurrections and repel invasions;

To provide for organizing, arming, and disciplining, the militia, and for governing such part of them as may be employed in the service of the United States, reserving to the states respectively, the appointment of the officers, and the authority of training the militia according to the discipline prescribed by Congress;

To exercise exclusive legislation in all cases whatsoever, over such District (not exceeding ten miles square) as may, by cession of particular states, and the acceptance of Congress, become the seat of the government of the United States, and to exercise like authority over all places purchased by the consent of the legislature of the state in which the same shall be, for the erection of forts, magazines, arsenals, dockyards, and other needful buildings;—And

To make all laws which shall be necessary and proper for carrying into execution the foregoing powers, and all other powers vested by this Constitution in the government of the United States, or in any department or officer thereof.

Section 9. The migration or importation of such persons as any of the states now existing shall think proper to admit, shall not be prohibited by the Congress prior to the year one thousand eight hundred and eight, but a tax or duty may be imposed on such importation, not exceeding ten dollars for each person.

The privilege of the writ of habeas corpus shall not be suspended, unless when in cases of rebellion or invasion the public safety may require it.

No bill of attainder or ex post facto Law shall be passed.

No capitation, or other direct, tax shall be laid, unless in proportion to the census or enumeration herein before directed to be taken.

No tax or duty shall be laid on articles exported from any state.

No preference shall be given by any regulation of commerce or revenue to the ports of one state over those of another: nor shall vessels bound to, or from, one state, be obliged to enter, clear or pay duties in another.

No money shall be drawn from the treasury, but in consequence of appropriations made by law; and a regular statement and account of receipts and expenditures of all public money shall be published from time to time.

No title of nobility shall be granted by the United States: and no person holding any office of profit or trust under them, shall, without the consent of the Congress, accept of any present, emolument, office, or title, of any kind whatever, from any king, prince, or foreign state.

Section 10. No state shall enter into any treaty, alliance, or confederation; grant letters of marque and reprisal; coin money; emit bills of credit; make anything but gold and silver coin a tender in payment of debts; pass any bill of attainder, ex post facto law, or law impairing the obligation of contracts, or grant any title of nobility.

No state shall, without the consent of the Congress, lay any imposts or duties on imports or exports, except what may be absolutely necessary for executing its inspection laws: and the net produce of all duties and imposts, laid by any state on imports or exports, shall be for the use of the treasury of the United States; and all such laws shall be subject to the revision and control of the Congress.

No state shall, without the consent of Congress, lay any duty of tonnage, keep troops, or ships of war in time of peace, enter into any agreement or compact with another state, or with a foreign power, or engage in war, unless actually invaded, or in such imminent danger as will not admit of delay.

Article II

Section 1. The executive power shall be vested in a President of the United States of America. He shall hold his office during the term of four years, and, together with the Vice President, chosen for the same term, be elected, as follows:

Each state shall appoint, in such manner as the Legislature thereof may direct, a number of electors, equal to the whole number of Senators and Representatives to which the State may be entitled in the Congress: but no Senator or Representative, or person holding an office of trust or profit under the United States, shall be appointed an elector.

The electors shall meet in their respective states, and vote by ballot for two persons, of whom one at least shall not be an inhabitant of the same state with themselves. And they shall make a list of all the persons voted for, and of the number of votes for each; which list they shall sign and certify, and transmit sealed to the seat of the government of the United States, directed to the President of the Senate. The President of the Senate shall, in the presence of the Senate and House of Representatives, open all the certificates, and the votes shall then be counted. The person having the greatest number of votes shall be the President, if such number be a majority of the whole number of electors appointed; and if there be more than one who have such majority, and have an equal number of votes, then the House of Representatives shall immediately choose by ballot one of them for President; and if no person have a majority, then from the five highest on the list the said House shall in like manner choose the President. But in choosing the President, the votes shall be taken by States, the representation from each state having one vote; A quorum for this purpose shall consist of a member or members from two thirds of the states, and a majority of all the states shall be necessary to a choice. In every case, after the choice of the President, the person having the greatest number of votes of the electors shall be the Vice President. But if there should remain two or more who have equal votes, the Senate shall choose from them by ballot the Vice President.

The Congress may determine the time of choosing the electors, and the day on which they shall give their votes; which day shall be the same throughout the United States.

No person except a natural born citizen, or a citizen of the United States, at the time of the adoption of this Constitution, shall be eligible to the office of President; neither shall any person be eligible to that office who shall not have attained to the age of thirty five years, and been fourteen Years a resident within the United States.

In case of the removal of the President from office, or of his death, resignation, or inability to discharge the powers and duties of the said office, the same shall devolve on the Vice President, and the Congress may by law provide for the case of removal, death, resignation or inability, both of the President and Vice President, declaring what officer shall then act as President, and such officer shall act accordingly, until the disability be removed, or a President shall be elected.

The President shall, at stated times, receive for his services, a compensation, which shall neither be increased nor diminished during the period for which he shall have been elected, and he shall not receive within that period any other emolument from the United States, or any of them.

Before he enter on the execution of his office, he shall take the following oath or affirmation: — "I do solemnly swear (or affirm) that I will faithfully execute the office of President of the United States, and will to the best of my ability, preserve, protect and defend the Constitution of the United States."

Section 2. The President shall be commander in chief of the Army and Navy of the United States, and of the militia of the several states, when called into the actual service of the United States; he may require the opinion, in writing, of the principal officer in each of the executive departments, upon any subject relating to the duties of their respective offices, and he shall have power to grant reprieves and pardons for offenses against the United States, except in cases of impeachment.

He shall have power, by and with the advice and consent of the Senate, to make treaties, provided two thirds of the Senators present concur; and he shall nominate, and by and with the advice and consent of the Senate, shall appoint ambassadors, other public ministers and consuls, judges of the Supreme Court, and all other officers of the United States, whose appointments are not herein otherwise provided for, and which shall be established by law: but the Congress may by law vest the appointment of such inferior officers, as they think proper, in the President alone, in the courts of law, or in the heads of departments.

The President shall have power to fill up all vacancies that may happen during the recess of the Senate, by granting commissions which shall expire at the end of their next session.

Section 3. He shall from time to time give to the Congress information of the state of the union, and recommend to their consideration such measures as he shall judge necessary and expedient; he may, on extraordinary occasions, convene both Houses, or either of them, and in case of disagreement between them, with respect to the time of adjournment, he may adjourn them to such time as he shall think proper; he shall receive ambassadors and other public ministers; he shall take care that the laws be faithfully executed, and shall commission all the officers of the United States.

Section 4. The President, Vice President and all civil officers of the United States, shall be removed from office on impeachment for, and conviction of, treason, bribery, or other high crimes and misdemeanors.

Article III

Section 1. The judicial power of the United States, shall be vested in one Supreme Court, and in such inferior courts as the Congress may from time to time ordain and establish. The judges, both of the supreme and inferior courts, shall hold their offices during good behaviour, and shall, at stated times, receive for their services, a compensation, which shall not be diminished during their continuance in office.

Section 2. The judicial power shall extend to all cases, in law and equity, arising under this Constitution, the laws of the United States, and treaties made, or which shall be made, under their authority; — to all cases affecting ambassadors, other public ministers and consuls; — to all cases of admiralty and maritime jurisdiction; — to controversies to which the United States shall be a party; — to controversies between two or more states; — between a state and citizens of another state; — between citizens of different states; — between citizens of the same state claiming lands under grants of different states, and between a state, or the citizens thereof, and foreign states, citizens or subjects.

In all cases affecting ambassadors, other public ministers and consuls, and those in which a state shall be party, the Supreme Court shall have original jurisdiction. In all the other cases before mentioned, the Supreme Court shall have appellate jurisdiction, both as to law and fact, with such exceptions, and under such regulations as the Congress shall make.

The trial of all crimes, except in cases of impeachment, shall be by jury; and such trial shall be held in the state where the said crimes shall have been committed; but when not committed within any state, the trial shall be at such place or places as the Congress may by law have directed.

Section 3. Treason against the United States, shall consist only in levying war against them, or in adhering to their enemies, giving them aid and comfort. No person shall be convicted of treason unless on the testimony of two witnesses to the same overt act, or on confession in open court.

The Congress shall have power to declare the punishment of treason, but no attainder of treason shall work corruption of blood, or forfeiture except during the life of the person attainted.

Article IV

Section 1. Full faith and credit shall be given in each state to the public acts, records, and judicial proceedings of every other state. And the Congress may by general laws prescribe the manner in which such acts, records, and proceedings shall be proved, and the effect thereof.

Section 2. The citizens of each state shall be entitled to all privileges and immunities of citizens in the several states.

A person charged in any state with treason, felony, or other crime, who shall flee from justice, and be found in another state, shall on demand of the executive authority of the state from which he fled, be delivered up, to be removed to the state having jurisdiction of the crime.

No person held to service or labor in one state, under the laws thereof, escaping into another, shall, in consequence of any law or regulation therein, be discharged from such service or labor, but shall be delivered up on claim of the party to whom such service or labor may be due.

Section 3. New states may be admitted by the Congress into this union; but no new states shall be formed or erected within the jurisdiction of any other state; nor any state be formed by the junction of two or more states, or parts of states, without the consent of the legislatures of the states concerned as well as of the Congress.

The Congress shall have power to dispose of and make all needful rules and regulations respecting the territory or other property belonging to the United States; and nothing in this Constitution shall be so construed as to prejudice any claims of the United States, or of any particular state.

Section 4. The United States shall guarantee to every state in this union a republican form of government, and shall protect each of them against invasion; and on application of the legislature, or of the executive (when the legislature cannot be convened) against domestic violence.

Article V

The Congress, whenever two thirds of both houses shall deem it necessary, shall propose amendments to this Constitution, or, on the application of the legislatures of two thirds of the several states, shall call a convention for proposing amendments, which, in either case, shall be valid to all intents and purposes, as part of this Constitution, when ratified by the legislatures of three fourths of the several states, or by conventions in three fourths thereof, as the one or the other mode of ratification may be proposed by the Congress; provided that no amendment which may be made prior to the year one thousand eight hundred and eight shall in any manner affect the first and fourth clauses in the ninth section of the first article; and that no state, without its consent, shall be deprived of its equal suffrage in the Senate.

Article VI

All debts contracted and engagements entered into, before the adoption of this Constitution, shall be as valid against the United States under this Constitution, as under the Confederation.

This Constitution, and the laws of the United States which shall be made in pursuance thereof; and all treaties made, or which shall be made, under the authority of the United States, shall be the supreme law of the land; and the judges in every state shall be bound thereby, anything in the Constitution or laws of any State to the contrary notwithstanding.

The Senators and Representatives before mentioned, and the members of the several state legislatures, and all executive and judicial officers, both of the United States and of the several states, shall be bound by oath or affirmation, to support this Constitution; but no religious test shall ever be required as a qualification to any office or public trust under the United States.

Article VII

The ratification of the conventions of nine states, shall be sufficient for the establishment of this Constitution between the states so ratifying the same.

Amendment I (1791)
Congress shall make no law respecting an establishment of religion, or prohibiting the free exercise thereof; or abridging the freedom of speech, or of the press; or the right of the people peaceably to assemble, and to petition the government for a redress of grievances.

Amendment II (1791)
A well regulated militia, being necessary to the security of a free state, the right of the people to keep and bear arms, shall not be infringed.

Amendment III (1791)
No soldier shall, in time of peace be quartered in any house, without the consent of the owner, nor in time of war, but in a manner to be prescribed by law.

Amendment IV (1791)
The right of the people to be secure in their persons, houses, papers, and effects, against unreasonable searches and seizures, shall

not be violated, and no warrants shall issue, but upon probable cause, supported by oath or affirmation, and particularly describing the place to be searched, and the persons or things to be seized.

Amendment V (1791)
No person shall be held to answer for a capital, or otherwise infamous crime, unless on a presentment or indictment of a grand jury, except in cases arising in the land or naval forces, or in the militia, when in actual service in time of war or public danger; nor shall any person be subject for the same offense to be twice put in jeopardy of life or limb; nor shall be compelled in any criminal case to be a witness against himself, nor be deprived of life, liberty, or property, without due process of law; nor shall private property be taken for public use, without just compensation.

Amendment VI (1791)
In all criminal prosecutions, the accused shall enjoy the right to a speedy and public trial, by an impartial jury of the state and district wherein the crime shall have been committed, which district shall have been previously ascertained by law, and to be informed of the nature and cause of the accusation; to be confronted with the witnesses against him; to have compulsory process for obtaining witnesses in his favor, and to have the assistance of counsel for his defense.

Amendment VII (1791)
In suits at common law, where the value in controversy shall exceed twenty dollars, the right of trial by jury shall be preserved, and no fact tried by a jury, shall be otherwise reexamined in any court of the United States, than according to the rules of the common law.

Amendment VIII (1791)
Excessive bail shall not be required, nor excessive fines imposed, nor cruel and unusual punishments inflicted.

Amendment IX (1791)
The enumeration in the Constitution, of certain rights, shall not be construed to deny or disparage others retained by the people.

Amendment X (1791)
The powers not delegated to the United States by the Constitution, nor prohibited by it to the states, are reserved to the states respectively, or to the people.

Amendment XI (1798)
The judicial power of the United States shall not be construed to extend to any suit in law or equity, commenced or prosecuted against one of the United States by citizens of another state, or by citizens or subjects of any foreign state.

Amendment XII (1804)
The electors shall meet in their respective states and vote by ballot for President and Vice-President, one of whom, at least, shall not be an inhabitant of the same state with themselves; they shall name in their ballots the person voted for as President, and in distinct ballots the person voted for as Vice-President, and they shall make distinct lists of all persons voted for as President, and of all persons voted for as Vice-President, and of the number of votes for each, which lists they shall sign and certify, and transmit sealed to the seat of the government of the United States, directed to the President of the Senate; — The President of the Senate shall, in the presence of the Senate and House of Representatives, open all the certificates and the votes shall then be counted; — the person having the greatest number of votes for President, shall be the President, if such number be a majority of the whole number of electors appointed; and if no person have such majority, then from the persons having the highest numbers not exceeding three on the list of those voted for as President, the House of Representatives shall choose immediately, by ballot, the President. But in choosing the President, the votes shall be taken by states, the representation from each state having one vote; a quorum for this purpose shall consist of a member or members from two-thirds of the states, and a majority of all the states shall be necessary to a

choice. And if the House of Representatives shall not choose a President whenever the right of choice shall devolve upon them, before the fourth day of March next following, then the Vice-President shall act as President, as in the case of the death or other constitutional disability of the President. The person having the greatest number of votes as Vice-President, shall be the Vice-President, if such number be a majority of the whole number of electors appointed, and if no person have a majority, then from the two highest numbers on the list, the Senate shall choose the Vice-President; a quorum for the purpose shall consist of two-thirds of the whole number of Senators, and a majority of the whole number shall be necessary to a choice. But no person consti-tutionally ineligible to the office of President shall be eligible to that of Vice-President of the United States.

Amendment XIII (1865)
Section 1. Neither slavery nor involuntary servitude, except as a punishment for crime whereof the party shall have been duly convicted, shall exist within the United States, or any place subject to their jurisdiction.

Section 2. Congress shall have power to enforce this article by ap-propriate legislation.

Amendment XIV (1868)
Section 1. All persons born or naturalized in the United States, and subject to the jurisdiction thereof, are citizens of the United States and of the state wherein they reside. No state shall make or enforce any law which shall abridge the privileges or immunities of citizens of the United States; nor shall any state deprive any person of life, liberty, or property, without due process of law; nor deny to any person within its jurisdiction the equal protection of the laws.
Section 2. Representatives shall be apportioned among the several states according to their respective numbers, counting the whole number of persons in each state, excluding Indians not taxed. But when the right to vote at any election for the choice of electors for

President and Vice President of the United States, Representatives in Congress, the executive and judicial officers of a state, or the members of the legislature thereof, is denied to any of the male inhabitants of such state, being twenty-one years of age, and citizens of the United States, or in any way abridged, except for participation in rebellion, or other crime, the basis of representation therein shall be reduced in the proportion which the number of such male citizens shall bear to the whole number of male citizens twenty-one years of age in such state.

Section 3. No person shall be a Senator or Representative in Congress, or elector of President and Vice President, or hold any office, civil or military, under the United States, or under any state, who, having previously taken an oath, as a member of Congress, or as an officer of the United States, or as a member of any state legislature, or as an executive or judicial officer of any state, to support the Constitution of the United States, shall have engaged in insurrection or rebellion against the same, or given aid or comfort to the enemies thereof. But Congress may by a vote of two-thirds of each House, remove such disability.

Section 4. The validity of the public debt of the United States, authorized by law, including debts incurred for payment of pensions and bounties for services in suppressing insurrection or rebellion, shall not be questioned. But neither the United States nor any state shall assume or pay any debt or obligation incurred in aid of insurrection or rebellion against the United States, or any claim for the loss or emancipation of any slave; but all such debts, obligations and claims shall be held illegal and void.

Section 5. The Congress shall have power to enforce, by appropriate legislation, the provisions of this article.

Amendment XV (1870)
Section 1. The right of citizens of the United States to vote shall not be denied or abridged by the United States or by any state on account of race, color, or previous condition of servitude.

Section 2. The Congress shall have power to enforce this article by appropriate legislation.

Amendment XVI (1913)

The Congress shall have power to lay and collect taxes on incomes, from whatever source derived, without apportionment among the several states, and without regard to any census of enumeration.

Amendment XVII (1913)

The Senate of the United States shall be composed of two Senators from each state, elected by the people thereof, for six years; and each Senator shall have one vote. The electors in each state shall have the qualifications requisite for electors of the most numerous branch of the state legislatures.

When vacancies happen in the representation of any state in the Senate, the executive authority of such state shall issue writs of election to fill such vacancies: Provided, that the legislature of any state may empower the executive thereof to make temporary appointments until the people fill the vacancies by election as the legislature may direct.

This amendment shall not be so construed as to affect the election or term of any Senator chosen before it becomes valid as part of the Constitution.

Amendment XVIII (1919)

Section 1. After one year from the ratification of this article the manufacture, sale, or transportation of intoxicating liquors within, the importation thereof into, or the exportation thereof from the United States and all territory subject to the jurisdiction thereof for beverage purposes is hereby prohibited.

Section 2. The Congress and the several states shall have concurrent power to enforce this article by appropriate legislation.

Section 3. This article shall be inoperative unless it shall have been ratified as an amendment to the Constitution by the legislatures of the several states, as provided in the Constitution, within seven years from the date of the submission hereof to the states by the Congress.

Amendment XIX (1920)
The right of citizens of the United States to vote shall not be denied or abridged by the United States or by any state on account of sex.

Congress shall have power to enforce this article by appropriate legislation.

Amendment XX (1933)
Section 1. The terms of the President and Vice President shall end at noon on the 20th day of January, and the terms of Senators and Representatives at noon on the 3d day of January, of the years in which such terms would have ended if this article had not been ratified; and the terms of their successors shall then begin.

Section 2. The Congress shall assemble at least once in every year, and such meeting shall begin at noon on the 3d day of January, unless they shall by law appoint a different day.

Section 3. If, at the time fixed for the beginning of the term of the President, the President elect shall have died, the Vice President elect shall become President. If a President shall not have been chosen before the time fixed for the beginning of his term, or if the President elect shall have failed to qualify, then the Vice President elect shall act as President until a President shall have qualified; and the Congress may by law provide for the case wherein neither a President elect nor a Vice President elect shall have qualified, declaring who shall then act as President, or the manner in which one who is to act shall be selected, and such person shall act accordingly until a President or Vice President shall have qualified.

Section 4. The Congress may by law provide for the case of the death of any of the persons from whom the House of Representatives may choose a President whenever the right of choice shall have devolved upon them, and for the case of the death of any of the persons from whom the Senate may choose a Vice President whenever the right of choice shall have devolved upon them.

Section 5. Sections 1 and 2 shall take effect on the 15th day of October following the ratification of this article.

Section 6. This article shall be inoperative unless it shall have been ratified as an amendment to the Constitution by the legislatures of three-fourths of the several states within seven years from the date of its submission.

Amendment XXI (1933)
Section 1. The eighteenth article of amendment to the Constitution of the United States is hereby repealed.

Section 2. The transportation or importation into any state, territory, or possession of the United States for delivery or use therein of intoxicating liquors, in violation of the laws thereof, is hereby prohibited.

Section 3. This article shall be inoperative unless it shall have been ratified as an amendment to the Constitution by conventions in the several states, as provided in the Constitution, within seven years from the date of the submission hereof to the states by the Congress.

Amendment XXII (1951)
Section 1. No person shall be elected to the office of the President more than twice, and no person who has held the office of President, or acted as President, for more than two years of a term to which some other person was elected President shall be elected to the office of the President more than once. But this article shall not apply to any person holding the office of President when this arti-

cle was proposed by the Congress, and shall not prevent any person who may be holding the office of President, or acting as President, during the term within which this article becomes operative from holding the office of President or acting as President during the remainder of such term.

Section 2. This article shall be inoperative unless it shall have been ratified as an amendment to the Constitution by the legislatures of three-fourths of the several states within seven years from the date of its submission to the states by the Congress.

Amendment XXIII (1961)
Section 1. The District constituting the seat of government of the United States shall appoint in such manner as the Congress may direct:

A number of electors of President and Vice President equal to the whole number of Senators and Representatives in Congress to which the District would be entitled if it were a state, but in no event more than the least populous state; they shall be in addition to those appointed by the states, but they shall be considered, for the purposes of the election of President and Vice President, to be electors appointed by a state; and they shall meet in the District and perform such duties as provided by the twelfth article of amendment.

Section 2. The Congress shall have power to enforce this article by appropriate legislation.

Amendment XXIV (1964)
Section 1. The right of citizens of the United States to vote in any primary or other election for President or Vice President, for electors for President or Vice President, or for Senator or Representative in Congress, shall not be denied or abridged by the United States or any state by reason of failure to pay any poll tax or other tax.

Section 2. The Congress shall have power to enforce this article by appropriate legislation.

Amendment XXV (1967)

Section 1. In case of the removal of the President from office or of his death or resignation, the Vice President shall become President.

Section 2. Whenever there is a vacancy in the office of the Vice President, the President shall nominate a Vice President who shall take office upon confirmation by a majority vote of both Houses of Congress.

Section 3. Whenever the President transmits to the President pro tempore of the Senate and the Speaker of the House of Representatives his written declaration that he is unable to discharge the powers and duties of his office, and until he transmits to them a written declaration to the contrary, such powers and duties shall be discharged by the Vice President as Acting President.

Section 4. Whenever the Vice President and a majority of either the principal officers of the executive departments or of such other body as Congress may by law provide, transmit to the President pro tempore of the Senate and the Speaker of the House of Representatives their written declaration that the President is unable to discharge the powers and duties of his office, the Vice President shall immediately assume the powers and duties of the office as Acting President.

Thereafter, when the President transmits to the President pro tempore of the Senate and the Speaker of the House of Representatives his written declaration that no inability exists, he shall resume the powers and duties of his office unless the Vice President and a majority of either the principal officers of the executive department or of such other body as Congress may by law provide, transmit within four days to the President pro tempore of the Senate and the Speaker of the House of Representatives their written declaration that the President is unable to discharge the powers and duties of his office. Thereupon Congress shall decide the issue, assembling within forty-eight hours for that purpose if not in session. If the Congress, within twenty-one days after receipt of the latter written declaration, or, if Congress is not in session, within twenty-one days after Congress is required to assemble, determines by two-thirds vote of both Houses that the President is unable to discharge the powers and duties of his office, the Vice President shall continue to discharge the same as Acting President; otherwise, the President shall resume the powers and duties of his office.

Amendment XXVI (1971)
Section 1. The right of citizens of the United States, who are 18 years of age or older, to vote, shall not be denied or abridged by the United States or any state on account of age.

Section 2. The Congress shall have the power to enforce this article by appropriate legislation.

Amendment XXVII (1992)
No law varying the compensation for the services of the Senators and Representatives shall take effect until an election of Representatives shall have intervened.

GLOSSARY

amici curiae. Friend of the court. Someone not directly involved in a court case can sometimes make an argument as a friend of the court.

bills of attainder. Punishment by legislative enactment rather than through the courts.

certiorari. A writ from a superior court to an subordinate court asking for a record of the case. Persons desiring to have their case heard by the Supreme Court ask the Supreme Court for a writ of certiorari, meaning they want the Court to get a copy of the case record so they can hear the case.

citizenship. Not defined until the Fourteenth Amendment. As of 1868, a citizen is anyone "born or naturalized in the United States, and subject to the jurisdiction thereof."

chancery. A court of equity — following a jurisprudence based on fairness rather than following the common law.

cloture. A device for shutting off unlimited debate in the United States Senate. See filibuster.

Common Law. Judge-made law common to the realm. This is law not passed by any legislature but emerging from judicial precedents.

constitutionalism. A constitution is a set of rules limiting the power of government and the people acting through their government. Constitutionalism is the belief that one is limited by a constitution.

coverture. The state of a married woman.

democracy. Madison defined democracy as a system of government where every citizen participates in making public decisions.

duces tecum. A writ demanding that someone bring documents or evidence to court.

executive order. The president can issue an executive order which, when published in the *Federal Register*, has the force of law.

ex parte. Apart from. A judicial proceeding involving only one party.

ex post facto. Done after the fact. An ex post facto law seeks to punish crimes committed before passage of the law.

federalism. A system of government whereby sovereignty is divided, with provincial authorities having authority over some questions.

filibuster. In the U.S. Senate members have the right of unlimited debate. A speech designed to stop action is called a filibuster.

habeas corpus. Have the body. This is a writ allowing a prisoner to challenge his or her incarceration by forcing his or her jailors to appear in court with evidence justifying the imprisonment.

judicial review. When the Supreme Court examines a law to determine if it is constitutional or not, it judicially reviews the law.

libel. To damage the reputation of another is to libel them.

natural law. Law emerging from nature rather than from legislative or judicial process.

penumbras. Something shadowy or indefinite. The Supreme Court has found rights implied or suggested in the Bill of Rights in addition to those overtly articulated.

per curiam. By the court. A decision said to be issued by the whole court rather than any particular judge.

police power. The states' powers to make and enforce laws for the health and safety of their citizens.

Political Action Committee (PAC). A fund raising group.

republic. A system of government where the citizens elect a few to make decisions for the whole. Madison contrasted this with a democracy, where all the citizens make decisions.

sovereignty. Ultimate power in government.

stare decisis . The rule that courts should obey their precedents.

writ of mandamus. A writ commanding someone or some agency to do something.

INDEX

TEACHING TEXTS IN LAW AND POLITICS ⚖

David Schultz, *General Editor*

The new series Teaching Texts in Law and Politics is devoted to textbooks that explore the multidimensional and multidisciplinary areas of law and politics. Special emphasis will be given to textbooks written for the undergraduate classroom. Subject matters to be addressed in this series include, but will not be limited to: constitutional law; civil rights and liberties issues; law, race, gender, and gender orientation studies; law and ethics; women and the law; judicial behavior and decision-making; legal theory; comparative legal systems; criminal justice; courts and the political process; and other topics on the law and the political process that would be of interest to undergraduate curriculum and education. Submission of single-author and collaborative studies, as well as collections of essays are invited.

Authors wishing to have works considered for this series should contact:

Peter Lang Publishing
Acquisitions Department
275 Seventh Avenue, 28th floor
New York, New York 10001

To order other books in this series, please contact our Customer Service Department at:

800-770-LANG (within the U.S.)
(212) 647-7706 (outside the U.S.)
(212) 647-7707 FAX

or browse online by series at:

WWW.PETERLANGUSA.COM